with Russell Stannard

Inside Out

Workbook

MACMILLAN

Macmillan Education
Between Towns Road, Oxford OX4 3PP, UK
A division of Macmillan Publishers Limited
Companies and representatives throughout the world

ISBN 0 333 92341 3 (International Edition)
ISBN 0 333 96744 5 (Level V)

Designed by Sarah Nicholson
Illustrated by Ray and Corrine Burroughs p 62; Martin Chatterton pp 18,
25, 46; Julian Mosedale pp 9, 26; Nicola Slater p 57
Cover design by Andrew Oliver
Cover painting *Chinoiserie* © Howard Hodgkin.

The authors and publishers would like to thank the following for
permission to reproduce their copyright material: Overseas Filmgroup
Inc. for the extract from the summary of the film Waking Ned on page 30
from http://www.ofg.com/films/waking_ned.text01.html; Heather
Clisby for the internet movie review on page 31 from
http://www.shoestring.org/mmi_revs/neddevine.html. Bocu Music Ltd
and Music Sales Ltd for one line from *Take a Chance on Me* on page 32,
words and music by Benny Andersson/Björn Ulvaeus, © Union Songs
AB, Stockholm, Sweden and Universal Music Publishing Ltd, 77 Fulham
Palace Road, London, W6 1977, reprinted by permission of Bocu Music
Ltd and Music Sales Ltd on behalf of the publishers. All Rights reserved;
Screen Gems-EMI Music Ltd, London, WC2H 0QY and Chelsea Music
Publishing for one line from *Always on my Mind* on page 32, words and
music by John Christopher, Mark James and Wayne Thompson, © Screen
Gems-EMI Music Inc/Sebanine Music Inc, USA 1971; Sony/ATV Music
Publishing for one line from *Suspicious Minds* on page 32, written by F.
Zambon; Peer Music (UK) Ltd and Music Sales Ltd for one line from
Sunshine Superman on page 32, words and music by Donovan Leitch, ©
Donovan (Music) Ltd 1966. All rights reserved; Western Mail & Echo Ltd
for the extract on page 55 from *Time and Tide Wait for No Man But
Bluebird Still Hits 128mph (206kph)* by Steve Dube from Western Mail
19.6.00, copyright © Western Mail & Echo Ltd 2000; The Grand Appeal
for the extract on page 73 from www.wrongtrousersday.btinternet.co.uk.

Whilst every effort has been made to locate the owners of copyright, in
some cases this has been unsuccessful. The publishers apologise for any
infringement or failure to acknowledge the original sources and will be
glad to include any necessary correction in subsequent printings.

The authors and publishers would like to thank the following for
permission to reproduce their photographs: Courtesy of The Grand
Appeal p73; Philly Page for BBC (Castaway Christmas Diary) p42;
George Bodnar/ Comic Relief Ltd p72; Corbis pp11, 54, 63, Bettman
pp41,43, Hulton pp4, 19, 21; Ronald Grant Cinema Archive/ Twentieth
Century Fox p30, Rank p58; Courtesy of Luke Kennedy p7; Liam Duke/
TimeOut Camera Press, London p8; Rex Features pp10, 32, 55; ©Becky
Ridding p14; Still Pictures p27; Stone p22; "Windjet, British wind
powered speed record craft. www.windjet.co.uk" p56

Commissioned photography by Haddon Davies p66

The publishers wish to thank BBC Radio Oxford, Jonathan Hancock and
Pippa Shay.

Printed and bound in Spain by Edelvives SA.

2005 2004 2003 2002
10 9 8 7 6 5 4 3

Contents

1 Identity

Quotes

Complete these quotes with *man* or *woman*.

a) 'If you want something said, ask a
_____man_____ ; if you want something done, ask
a _____woman_____ .' *Margaret Thatcher*

b) 'I don't mind living in a _____man_____ 's world
as long as I can be a _____woman_____ in it.'
Marilyn Monroe

Grammar

1 Read these sentences about the life of Marilyn
Monroe and underline the adverbials. There may
be more than one adverbial in some sentences.

a) Marilyn Monroe was born on 1st June 1926.

b) It's not known who her father was and her
mother had a history of mental problems,
which meant that Marilyn's childhood was
extremely difficult.

c) Marilyn was brought up in Los Angeles by
several different foster families.

d) Finally she entered an orphanage where she
lived until 1937.

e) After appearing in a promotional campaign
for the army she quickly became an extremely
popular model and appeared on the covers of
many famous magazines.

f) During her life Marilyn Monroe married three
times.

g) She divorced for the third time in 1961.

h) In the same year she was briefly hospitalised
in a mental clinic.

i) Tragically, Marilyn Monroe was found dead
on 4th August 1962.

2 Complete the text below with an appropriate
adverbial from the box.

> by Golden Globe   still   incredibly ✓
> in a period when TV was rapidly expanding

Marilyn Monroe became the focus of incredible
media attention (a) *in a period when TV was rapidly expanding*
She achieved enormous success and became
(b) _____incredibly_____ popular. In 1962
she was named the 'World's most popular star'
(c) _____by Golden Globe_____ and is
(d) _____still_____ considered to be
one of the world's sexiest pin-ups.

> in Westwood Memorial Park, Los Angeles ✓
> undoubtedly   at the age of 36   automatically ✓
> frequently

However, success didn't (e) _____automatically_____
bring her happiness. Her emotional instability was
probably the result of her very difficult and
traumatic childhood, but the fact that she was
(f) _____frequently_____ given parts that cast
her in a role too similar to the one she played in
real life was (g) _____undoubtedly_____ a
contributing factor. Marilyn Monroe died
(h) *in Westwood Memorial Park, Los Angeles*. She was laid to
rest (i) _____at the age of 36_____ .

3 Rewrite the sentences below, changing the position
of the adverbial in **bold** so that the meaning of the
sentence changes.

a) I had really wanted my boyfriend to meet my
parents **earlier on in the day.**
*Earlier on in the day I had really
wanted my boyfriend to meet my parents.*

b) **Frankly**, she just didn't answer the question.
She just didn't answer the question frankly.

c) I really regretted having asked Jane to come to
the party **later.**
*Later I really regretted having asked
Jane to come to the party.*

d) I'd just talk to him about it **normally.**
Normally, I'd just talk to him about it.

4 You are going to read a short conversation between two friends. These sentences have been taken from the conversation. Put them in the correct order.

a) moods / put / I / anymore / with / can't / his / up / just

I can't just put up with his moods anymore

b) really / whole / getting / situation / is / down / the / me /

The whole situation is really getting me down.

c) just / paper / starts / through / he / flicking / the

He just starts flicking through the paper.

d) like / things / does / bottling / no / up / that / good / it

It does no good bottling things up like that.

e) something / knew / we'd / with / come / I / up

I knew we'd come up with something.

f) help / someone / talk / might / it / to / it / with / through

It might help to talk it through with someone.

5 Use the sentences in 4 above to complete the conversation.

Mel: What's up Kate?

Kate: I'm sorry, I really don't want to talk about it.

Mel: Come on, you know (1) ___d___ .

Kate: Yes, I know, it's just that (2) ___b___ .

Mel: Go on, you know you can tell me about it and (3) ___f___ .

Kate: It's Pete, (4) ___a___ .

Mel: Have you talked to him about it?

Kate: Yes, but every time I try to start a serious conversation (5) ___c___ or something and I get really angry!

Mel: Well, how about writing him a letter, that way you've got time to think about what you want to say ...

Kate: Yeah, I suppose so, and maybe I won't get so angry, I suppose that would help ...

Mel: There you are, you see, (6) ___e___ !

Vocabulary

1 Circle the correct word.

a) The ability to be tactful is a great *skill* / *skilled* / *skilfulness*.

b) She works so *efficient* / *efficiency* / *efficiently* with her new computer that she gets the job done in half the time.

c) He's completely lacking in *competence* / *competent* / *competently* and can't do the job properly.

d) I'm looking for a job where I can *fulfilment* / *fulfil* / *fulfilling* my ambition to write.

e) It's very *satisfaction* / *satisfying* / *satisfied* when people congratulate you on making a good presentation.

f) He's got no *consideration* / *consider* / *considerate* for anyone, he just does what he wants and expects everyone to fit in with him.

g) Do you really think getting that report finished by five o'clock is *achievement* / *achievable* / *achievably*?

2 Complete the sentences with the correct form of the words in brackets.

a) She's a very _considerate_ person and always thinks about the needs of the people around her. (consideration)

b) I really don't think your work is _satisfactory_ . You're going to have to make much more effort if you hope to pass the exam. (satisfaction)

c) It really is one of the most _fulfilling_ jobs I have done. It's great to see the students making so much progress. (fulfilment)

d) I really don't feel that your son is _achieving_ as much as he could. He needs to take his studies a lot more seriously. (achievement)

e) The shortage of _skilled_ workers is a big problem at the moment. (skill)

f) That's not a very _efficient_ way of working. I'm sure you could do the job much faster. (efficiency)

g) He's a very _competent_ driver. He'll have no problem passing his test. (competence)

3 Complete Mel's e-mail message to Sue with the (phrasal verbs) from the box.

homework

to not allow other people to ... so that you are unhappy or angry.

| talk through | break off | sort out | bottle up |
| look into | get down | look up to | put up with |

to discuss *solution* *to find* *to depress* *to tolerate*

From: Mel   To: Sue
Subject: Kate

Hi Sue,

Have you heard the latest? Kate's (a) *broken off* her engagement with Pete! Can you believe it? I suppose she has had to (b) *put up with* a lot of nonsense from him recently, like that time he promised to (c) *sort out* her tax return for her and then completely forgot! And he always seems to be in a bad mood these days, It's a shame though, she really used to (d) *look up to* him at the beginning. The main problem is he just doesn't communicate. Kate tries her best, but he just refuses to (e) *talk* things *through* with her. He just keeps quiet, (f) *bottles* things *up* and I think Kate has just had enough. I think the whole thing's really (g) *getting* her *down*, she looked pretty upset when I saw her. Maybe you could give her a ring and try and cheer her up a bit?

Anyway, I've been (h) *looking into* the possibility of going to Paris for a long weekend. I picked up some brochures from the travel agent's yesterday. Why don't you come over tonight and see what you think?

Mel

homework

4 Rearrange these sentences to form a conversation between Amanda and her boyfriend Bill.

A: *Oh, it's you, is it? Do you know what time it is? You said you'd be over at seven and it's eight thirty!* 1

a) B: Listen, Amanda, I'm really sorry, but I honestly don't <u>fancy it</u> ... I've had a hellish day at work, and I'm really <u>stressed out</u> ... 8

b) A: Yes I am! That's just so typical of you to forget ... 5

c) B: Would you do that? You really don't care? 10

d) A: Had you forgotten we're going out tonight? It's Ruth's birthday ... 3

e) A: No, not at all. How about I <u>pick up</u> a video and a pizza and come round to your house and we just have a quiet night in? 11

f) B: Look, I'm really sorry, I just lost track of time ... 2

g) A: OK, OK, you're right ... let's just <u>drop it</u> shall we? So, are you coming or what? 7

h) B: Hey, come on now, you're a fine one to talk. What about last week? Eh? 6

i) A: Yeah, you sound a bit down ... do you want me to phone Ruth and make an excuse? 9

j) B: Ruth's birthday ... Yes, yes, of course it is, sorry love ... are you <u>really mad at me</u>? 4

B: *That sounds great! Thanks a lot love, you're an angel!* 12

homework

5 Match the <u>underlined</u> phrases in the dialogue with the definitions below.

a) stop talking about something *drop it*
b) collect *pick up*
c) tense and tired after a hard day's work *stressed out*
d) very angry (with someone) *really mad at so.*
e) like the idea of doing something *fancy it*

Pronunciation

1 🔲 Listen to the following sentences. Put a tick (✔) in the box if the speaker sounds angry.

a) Your problem is that you don't think things through. ✓

b) Don't let it get you down. She's just jealous. ☐

c) He's put up with her for 20 years and they're still married. ✓

d) I've got to sort out these files before I go home. ☐

e) I've only had time to flick through the report. ☐

f) Have you come up with anything yet? ✓

we stress the important meaning

2 Look at this short dialogue between a girlfriend and a boyfriend. They are both extremely angry. Mark the main stress in each sentence.

Kim: I can't <u>stand</u> it anymore! Why do you <u>always</u> have to do that?

Dan: Right, that's it! I've had enough. I'm out of here!

Kim: Good <u>riddance</u> ... and don't bother coming back!

Dan: Don't worry, I won't!

🔲 Listen to the dialogue to check your answers. Then repeat each line of the dialogue after the recording. Try to use the same angry tone as the speakers.

please sb. going.

Reading & listening

homework

1 Read the interview and match the questions to the answers. Be careful, there is one extra question.

- 2 a) What do you like about your job?
- 5 b) Would you recommend it to others?
- 1 c) How did you start working in the video industry?
- d) Do you think you will stay in the job in the future?
- 4 e) Did you need to have any special qualifications for the job?
- 3 f) What do you least like about the job?

Luke Kennedy

video industry?

e 1 _How did you start working in the_

Well, it wasn't something I really planned to do. I kind of <u>slipped into</u> it. A friend of mine needed some help carrying the cameras and stuff and basically it took off from there. It's amazing how quickly you <u>pick everything up</u>. One minute I seemed to be carrying the cameras around and the next minute I was going to Paris to shoot the fashion show.

a 2 _What do you like about your job?_

Well, the money's good. You can earn a packet when you're working. The trouble is you often have long periods when you're not working at all, so you have to organise things pretty well. To be honest, I'm not always that keen on the people I meet. Most people in the pop industry, especially the artists themselves, can be pretty awkward. They just want to <u>turn up</u>, do the shoot and <u>get off</u>. They start complaining when anything goes wrong. The trouble is you often have to take a certain scene about ten different times and that's when the frustration starts showing.

5 3 _What do you least like about the job?_

I hate the travelling. I know that might sound a bit odd but it means you have to sort out all the equipment and find local people to help you, and it can be a lot of bother. You end up spending most of the time organising trivial things, you might have problems with the location, the language and stuff. The worst thing is when you're filming in a cold country. I once worked in the north of Poland and I thought I was going to freeze to death. It's not like appearing in a video where you just arrive and do the job. You have to organise most things yourself and so travelling can be a real pain.

e 4 _Did you need to have any special qualifications for the job?_

It's funny really. I never studied for the job, well not at first anyway, but it does require quite a bit of technical know-how. Actually, with all this digital computer stuff, it's getting pretty complicated and so, in the end, I went to university to study digital video and film. I don't know if it's been worth the effort though.

b 5 _Would you recommend it to others?_

No, I wouldn't advise you to <u>get into</u> the industry. It's too unstable. One week you're earning a packet and then for the next month you haven't got any work. It's worse when you're in my shoes; I've got two children and a wife to <u>look after</u>.

homework

2 <u>Underline</u> the phrasal verbs in the interview. Then match them to these meanings:

- a) became successful very quickly _took off_
- b) learn by doing something directly, without studying _pick everything up_
- c) accidentally got involved in something _slipped into it_
- d) organise _sort out_
- e) leave _get off_
- f) find yourself in an unexpected situation _end up_
- g) arrive _turn up_
- h) support _look after_
- i) become involved _get into_

homework

3 Match words from column A with words from column B to make common phrases taken from Luke's interview. Then check your answers with the text.

A		B	
3 a)	freeze	1	my shoes
3 b)	sound	2	know-how
4 c)	worth	3	pain
4 d)	technical	4	a bit odd
3 e)	a real	5	to death
5 f)	in	6	the effort

4 Use the phrases in 3 on page 7 to complete these sentences. Make any changes that are necessary.

a) It may seem simple to you but if you were _in my shoes_ you might see things differently.

b) You're being _a real pain_. You haven't stopped complaining since you got up.

c) It was -4°C and I only had a thin jacket with me. I thought I was going to _freeze to death_.

d) You need a lot of _technical know-how_ to work in the film-making industry today.

e) Is something the matter with Tom? I spoke to him yesterday and he _sounded a bit odd_.

f) I don't know if it was really _worth the effort_ putting all those extra hours in for no extra pay.

5 You are going to listen to Gary, who is a single parent. Tick (✔) the points you think he might make.

a) It's easy to bring up children.

✗ b) There are certain things women naturally do better than men.

✔ c) Being a single dad changed the way I looked at parenthood.

✗ d) There's lots of sexism towards men as well.

✗ e) Being a single dad changed my relationship with my kids.

✗ f) I got lots of support from my family.

✔ g) I never have any free time for girlfriends.

h) My children have been affected by not having a mother in the house.

✔ i) I think I've done a good job.

✗ j) I'm an expert at sewing, cooking and ironing.

Listen to the interview to check. (If you don't have the recording, read the tapescript of the interview on page 78.)

6 Listen again and answer these questions.

a) Why did he have to look after the children? _His wife moved south because of work_

b) In what ways does Gary think that men and women are different? _Women pay attention to detail they are too organized, they take the fun out of life._

c) What does his wife think about the way he has brought up his children? _It was irresponsible because the girls joined in with him_

d) What did they do in Greece? _They camped for a week_

e) What type of things does Gary like to do with his children? _Holiday, housework, concerts, sport_

f) Why didn't his mother and father help him more? _He didn't need help._

g) Who is his latest girlfriend? _It's Sara's best friend's mother's sister._

Writing

homework

1 Read this text about best-selling novelist Alex Garland. Where would you expect to see this text?

- in an academic essay by a literature student
- in the introduction on the first page of his first novel
- in a newspaper book review of his first novel
- in a gossip column in a magazine

Alex Garland was born in London, England, in 1970. The son of cartoonist Nick Garland, he was brought up in a house where people concerned themselves with social and political issues and held strong views. His family encouraged him to travel and put no pressure on him to conform and settle down. After leaving school, he spent six months in south-east Asia, and he has returned every year since. His travels there have had an obvious influence on his first novel, which is set on the beautiful beaches of Thailand. In 1992, he received a BA in History of Art at Manchester University and hoped to carve out a profession for himself as a cartoonist, following in his father's footsteps. However, he quickly became more interested in narrative than drawing and, frustrated with the limitations of cartoon strips, decided to embark on his first novel. He states that he started writing fiction not out of compulsion, but as an alternative to the conventional careers that most of his friends had chosen, with the stressful, driven lifestyles that they entail. He lives in a flat in London and occasionally works as an illustrator and freelance journalist.

2 Which of this information is included in the text?

a) his family

b) his friends

c) his hometown

d) his school

e) his ambitions

f) his novel

g) his job before becoming a writer

h) his hopes and dreams as a child

i) his literary influences

j) his university education

3 You have just published your first novel, it is tipped to become a best-seller. Write a short profile of yourself to go on the first page of the paperback edition. Decide what you think your reading public would like to know about you. Remember to include details about:

your hometown   your job or studies
your family   your main influences

Now write your profile. You should write about 200 words. Make sure you write it in the third person.

2 Taste

Food idioms

1 Match these idioms to their correct meanings. Use a dictionary if you need to.

   a) the apple of your eye
   b) as cool as a cucumber
   c) cream of the crop
   d) cry over spilt milk
   e) eat humble pie
   f) full of beans
   g) in a nutshell
   h) nutty as a fruitcake
   i) a hard nut to crack
   j) your bread and butter

  g 1 briefly
  h 2 crazy
  f 3 energetic
  c 4 the best
  j 5 your main source of income
  i 6 a difficult problem
  e 7 apologise
  b 8 calm
  d 9 regret something that has already happened
  a 10 your favourite person, usually a child

2 Complete these sentences with idioms from 1. You will need to change the form of some of the idioms.

   a) Well, I'm an actor really, waiting on tables is just the way I earn _my bread and butter_ .

   b) I don't know how you can be so _full of beans_ at this time in the morning! I'm still half asleep!

   c) Look, there's absolutely no point in _crying over spilt milk_ . What's done is done, you just have to get on with life.

   d) Sally is _the apple of_ her grandmother's _eye_ . She's always spoiling her, giving her presents and taking her on outings.

   e) I've never seen anyone like him, he's always _as cool as a cucumber_. Nothing bothers him and he never, ever loses his temper.

Grammar

1 <u>Underline</u> **all** the noun phrases in the following description:

We had a great dinner. Lucy cooked for us, she's a fantastic cook. We started with these gorgeous little smoked salmon pancakes. They were absolutely delicious! Then we had some cold cucumber soup

and tiny little fingers of crisp toast. The main course was incredible, you really should have seen it. She brought out a tray of fresh lobster and served them up with a very simple green salad. I thought I couldn't possibly eat any more, but when she brought out the dessert, a home-made chocolate mousse, it was just too good to resist!

2 Reorder these words and phrases to form complex noun phrases to describe different types of drink.

   a) wine / with just a hint of vanilla / delicate / white / sweet / a
     a delicate sweet white wine with just a hint of vanilla

   b) piping hot / straight from the pot / tea / a cup of / lovely
     a cup of lovely piping hot tea straight from the pot.

   c) citric / a mixture of / with just a touch of / champagne / juices / tangy
     a mixture of tangy citric juices with just a touch of champagne.

   d) and a slice of lemon / water / with a couple of / fresh mint leaves / ice cold / a glass of
     a glass of ice cold water with a couple of fresh mint leaves and a slice of lemon.

   e) full-fat / straight from the fridge / a glass of / milk / fresh
     a glass of fresh, full-fat milk straight from the fridge..

   f) hot / on top / a steaming cup of / with a dollop of cream / chocolate
     a steaming cup of hot chocolate with a dollop of cream on top.

3 Rewrite these sentences, as in the example.

Example

He swam|along the river.
Along the river he swam.

a) The days when the baker would deliver fresh bread to your home are|long gone.

Long gone are the days when the baker would deliver fresh bread to your home.

b) The cat jumped up.

Up jumped the cat / Up the cat jumped.

c) His speciality is|Andalucian gastronomy.

Andalucian gastronomy is his speciality.

d) He flew|out of the house.

Out of the house he flew out.

e) His business is|banking.

Banking is his business.

4 Underline all the examples of fronting in the two texts below and then rewrite them in a more informal style.

a) With five minutes left it was still 0–0 and everything to play for. One of the Liverpool players went in with a hard tackle and down went Chelsea's star player Luca Romano, but not for long. Jumping to his feet, Luca got the ball, slipped past the last defender and kicked the ball as hard as he could. In went the ball and the crowd went mad. Chelsea 1 – Liverpool 0.

1 _____
_____

2 _____
_____

b) Gone are the days when the boss played God over an office of cowering underlings. Equality is the name of the game in today's business world, with everyone taking an equal share of the work and likewise an equal share of the responsibility, or at least that's what the gurus would have us believe.

1 _____
_____

2 _____
_____

Pronunciation

1 🔊 Listen to these people commenting on a fashion show. Decide if they:

a) definitely like the clothes

b) don't like them

1 A: So, what do you think of the pink jacket?
  B: Well, it's very unusual.

2 A: What about the Versace trousers?
  B: Um, they're not really what I expected.

3 A: What do you think of the grey suit?
  B: Oh, well, typically Armani.

4 A: And what about that Dolce and Gabbana swimsuit?
  B: The thing that particularly strikes me is the colour.

5 A: Do you like the winter coats?
  B: Well, they look nice and warm.

6 A: And the evening dress with the sequins?
  B: Er, my grandmother used to wear one just like that.

🔊 Listen again and mark the main stresses. Then read the dialogue along with the speakers in the recording.

2 Mark and Nick are discussing a new job offer Nick's just received. Look at Mark's questions. Do you think Nick answers *yes* or *no* to them?

a) So, you've definitely decided to resign, have you?   yes / no

b) Are you going to tell the boss today? yes / no

c) Well, are you going to take up that new job offer?   yes / no

d) Don't you like the sound of it?   yes / no

e) So the salary's the problem, then?   yes / no

3 🔊 Listen to the recording to check. Do Nick's answers sound certain or uncertain? Write C or U.

a) ____   b) ____   c) ____   d) ____   e) ____

🔊 Listen again and repeat the answers. Try to copy Nick's intonation as closely as possible.

homework.

Vocabulary

1 Match a word in column A to a word from column B to make phrases to do with food.

A		B	
a)	convenience	1	potatoes
b)	milk	2	burger
c)	mashed	3	biscuits
d)	roast	4	dressing
e)	crunchy	5	strawberries
f)	succulent	6	chocolate
g)	bitter	7	food
h)	plastic	8	coffee
i)	salad	9	cup
j)	greasy	10	lamb

2 Complete the text below with a word from the box. Use one of the words twice.

juice

appetite aromas dishes elaborate _complicated_
flavours raw spicy taste

The Japanese eat a lot of (a) _raw_ fish, often without any extra flavourings of any description. They also eat a lot of rice and their diet has been connected to the very low levels of heart disease that exist in Japan. Their food isn't especially (b) _elaborate_; it relies on good quality, fresh products. They often eat a variety of small (c) _dishes_ which are known as sushi. It is very popular in London and New York.

The funny thing about Chinese food is that it seems to (d) _taste_ different in every country you eat it in and yet nothing like the Chinese food you eat in China. In China there are hundreds of small restaurants that set up in the squares and streets during the evening. Cities like Peking are a hive of activity and the (e) _aromas_ from the restaurants really give you an (f) _appetite_.

Most people think that all Indian food is hot and (g) _spicy_. While some of it is, India is such a big country that the variety is absolutely phenomenal. The Indians like to leave their food in spices, herbs or sometimes in sauces overnight, so it soaks up their (h) _flavour_. One other surprising thing about Indian food is the colour. The meat often comes up in a sizzling deep red colour and the sauces are often a mixture of deep oranges, reds and yellows. Eating Indian food can take a bit of getting used to. But once you get a (i) _taste_ for it, you're hooked.

3 Replace a word or phrase in each sentence with a word or phrase from the box. _by starting or running businesses._

a person who makes money	
clientele batter entrepreneur thrust (v.) _push sth. violently or suddenly in a particular direction_
homely pricey sped off blared out
exquisite thriving _to become and continue to be successful, strong, healthy_
extremely beautiful and carefully made _to make a loud unpleasant noise_

a) It's a simple, comfortable and informal restaurant run by a family. _homely_

b) The food was fantastic – perfectly cooked and beautifully presented. _exquisite_

c) Our meal was spoilt by the music which played loudly from a loudspeaker above our table. _blared out_

d) That restaurant's far too expensive. Let's find somewhere else to eat. _pricey_ _thrust_

e) The customer violently pushed the plate into the waiter's hands and said, 'Take this away, it's disgusting!'. _thrust_

f) He runs a successful restaurant just outside Rome. _thriving_

g) The fish was coated in a mixture of flour, milk and egg whites, and then deep fried. _batter_

h) The new company was set up by a businessman with plenty of money and new ideas. _an entrepreneur_

i) The restaurant's regular customers come from far and wide. _clientele_

j) We jumped in the car and drove away quickly. _sped off_

4 Match the sentences in box A to their endings in box B.

A

> a) I think he's got great taste in clothes,
> b) I think that joke was in very bad taste,
> c) She works as a wine taster
> d) It's a place with something for all tastes
> e) Fresh fruit from Spain has so much taste,
> f) The main course was very tasty but
> g) I'm not quite sure about the taste,

B

> 1 it's a joy to go shopping at the fruit markets there.
> 2 it was offensive and certainly not funny.
> 3 perhaps it needs a bit more garlic.
> 4 he always looks so smart and elegant.
> 5 where all the family will find something to do.
> 6 I was disappointed with the dessert.
> 7 and spends most of her time in the vineyards of France.

e | b | g | a | d | f | c

5 Complete the sentences with words formed from *taste*.

a) The choice of colours was very
___tastful___ . It was obvious that whoever owned the house had a good eye for colours.

b) She works as a chocolate ___taster___ for a supermarket chain.

c) He thought the food ___tasted___ bland. It wasn't what he expected from such an expensive restaurant.

d) The beer festival normally starts quite seriously with everyone ___tating___ the different beers on offer and commenting on them.

e) I thought the whole wedding ceremony was ___tasteless___ . I mean who in their right mind would have a priest dressed as Elvis Presley?

f) That really was a ___tasty___ meal. I must remember to come here again.

g) She was clearly a very elegant woman. She was ___tastefully___ dressed in a grey jacket and black trousers.

Listening & reading

1 ▣▣ Cover the tapescript and listen to four stories about people's experiences in restaurants. Then choose an appropriate title for each one.

a) Open all hours
b) Waiter, waiter, there's a chef in my soup
c) A fishy tale
d) A free lunch

a) story ☐   b) story ☐
c) story ☐   d) story ☐

2 In which story is there:

a) a case of mistaken identity?
b) an illness?
c) a generous gesture?
d) a violent incident?

a) story ☐   b) story ☐
c) story ☐   d) story ☐

Now look at the tapescript to check your answers.

3 Which stories do these sentences come from?

a) It's great to see you. You know, Luis was asking after you. He was wondering if you were still working on that translation project.

b) Don't worry. I eat here all the time. Let me do the ordering.

c) I've had enough of this! I'm not going to stand for it any longer!

d) There's plenty of wine behind the bar and the music is by the stereo.

a) story ☐   b) story ☐
c) story ☐   d) story ☐

> 1 On our first date, my boyfriend took me to a really posh restaurant. Clearly wanting to impress me, he insisted on ordering, so I said fine, but warned him not to order anything with shellfish in it – I'm allergic to it. I thought I'd made myself perfectly clear about this and that he knew what he was ordering, but obviously he didn't. An hour later I was in an ambulance being rushed to hospital. I could hardly breathe. My boyfriend looked rather embarrassed sitting by my side holding the oxygen mask to my face.

2 We were sitting in a restaurant in Manchester when we noticed three guys on the next table who were obviously getting frustrated because the service was so slow. Suddenly one of them stood up and started shouting at the waiter and telling him to hurry up with his food. The waiter answered back rather rudely and the next minute everything went ballistic. One of the guys ran into the kitchen and started a fight with a chef and the other two began fighting with the waiters. It was like something out of a cowboy film with bodies flying everywhere. Finally, one of the chefs came flying across our table and ended up with his face in my soup. The crazy thing is they still made us pay the bill and we weren't even offered a discount.

3 I was in a restaurant with my wife one evening and I couldn't help noticing a couple waving to me from a different table. Eventually the man came over, he said hello and started talking about something I knew nothing about. He then said 'Goodbye Pablo' and sat back down at his table. We finished our meal and asked for the bill. The waiter told us that the man on the other table, who'd since left, had paid it for us. I'm absolutely certain I'd never met him in my life.

4 I used to live in a little village in Crete and each Friday my friends and I would go down to the port to eat at our favourite restaurant. The owner, Petros, was a lovely guy and when I told him my friend was coming over from England he said he'd put on a special night for us. And he certainly did. It was amazing, the food was out of this world. As the evening went on, we all started dancing, and when it got to twelve o'clock, Petros came up to me. I thought he was going to ask us to leave but instead he gave me the keys to the restaurant and told me we could stay as long as we liked providing we didn't forget to lock everything up!

f) … the man on the other table, who'd since left, had paid it for us.

g) I thought he was going to ask us to leave …

h) … as long as we didn't forget to lock everything up!

5 Complete column B with words from the box.

> the bill   a discount   the waiter   the menu
> a table for four

A	B
ask	the waiter
ask for	the bill, a discount, the waiter, a table for four
pay	the bill,
query	
offer	a discount
order from	the menu
look at	the menu, the bill, a table for four
call	the waiter,
tip	the waiter
book	a table for for

6 Complete the following text with verb and noun combinations from the table.

It hadn't been a bad night at all, we had (a) _____ at a small French restaurant just round the corner from my house. There was a wide range of dishes to choose from, but in the end we decided not to (b) _____ , but to go for the set meal. The service was a bit slow, and we had to (c) _____ over quite a few times before we managed to place our order. The food was very good, and so was the wine, but when it came to (d) _____ we were in for a nasty surprise: it was astronomical! We (e) _____ , but to no avail. We even (f) _____ , but the waiter just laughed at us. So there was nothing else for it, but to shut up, pay up and leave. Needless to say we didn't (g) _____ !

4 Look at the extracts below. Read the tapescript and decide what the underlined pronouns refer to.

a) I'm allergic to it. shellfish   allergic

b) … I'd made myself perfectly clear about this.

c) … telling him to hurry up with his food.   waiter

d) … the other two began fighting with the waiters.   three guys who were waiting for food / a couple

e) … he said hello and started talking about something I knew nothing about.

Writing

1 Read this review for a new restaurant that has just opened. Then answer these questions:

a) What kind of food does it serve?
b) What is the atmosphere like?
c) Is it expensive?

If you haven't been to Casa Paco yet, then you don't know what you're missing. This cosy little tapas bar has just opened on the High Street. It is set out like a farmhouse kitchen, with simple pine furniture, traditional Spanish earthenware and a huge fire blazing in the grate. The atmosphere is laid-back and friendly and the clientele a mixture of students, young professionals and friends of the Spanish couple who run the place. The menu offers an incredibly wide selection of dishes ranging from classic tortillas to the exquisite daily specials conjured up on the spot by Paco and his wife Laura. The quality of the food is superb, a difficult task with such an amazing range of delicacies to choose from. We tried more than fifteen dishes between us, each one better than the last. The shellfish is so fresh you can still smell the sea, the meat succulent and done to a turn, the sweets quite something to behold. It can get quite busy at the weekend, but the staff are never flustered and it's always service with a smile. Perhaps the secret lies in the smooth Latin sounds playing softly in the background. All this for the price of your average pizza. If you're looking for a new eating experience, head for Casa Paco. You won't be disappointed!

2 You were so impressed by the review that you decided to book a table at Casa Paco for a surprise birthday party for a very close friend. The evening was a total disaster. Look at the list below and choose four or five of the problems to describe your evening.

- more than half the dishes on the menu were unavailable
- there were no daily specials
- the fish was off and had to be sent back
- the waiters were surly

- the service was incredibly slow
- the restaurant was packed
- you had to wait three quarters of an hour for your table
- you were expected to share a table with another group of people
- some of the dishes were cold by the time they arrived on the table
- it was very expensive – definitely over-priced!

3 You are going to write a letter of complaint to the magazine the review appeared in. Before you do, read a letter written by another angry reader, complaining about a recent film review printed in the same magazine and answer these questions.

a) What was the review for?
b) Why is the writer of the letter so angry?

Having recently read a rave review in your magazine for the latest John Howard film, I immediately phoned my local cinema and booked three tickets for myself and two friends. We were looking forward to a great evening, but I'm sad to say that we were grievously disappointed.

Your reviewer had described the film as a 'fun-packed adventure story' and we had gone in the hope of taking our minds off the stresses and strains of a hard week at work. It turned out that the film was far from light-hearted. The plot was depressing; the story of a young man fighting a life-threatening disease, the film itself long and very slow-moving and the ending one of the saddest I've ever seen at the cinema. In brief, the review was totally misleading. The film itself is very good, but I would only recommend it for those looking for a real tear-jerker.

I'm sorry to say that after such an awful experience I don't think I'll ever be able to trust your reviews again. I suggest you take more care in the future or you will lose more loyal readers like myself.

Yours disappointedly,
Rob Walters

4 Read the letter again and <u>underline</u> any useful language that you think you could use in your letter. Follow the same paragraph structure as in the model letter above and write your letter of complaint. You should write about 200 words.

3 City

Anagrams

Rearrange the letters to spell out the names of eight cities, then match the cities to the clues below.

a) nacbalero _blacerona_   e) epgrua _prague_
b) coeixm tyic _mexico city_   f) kooyt _kyoto_
c) dbenihrgu _edimburgh_   g) goacich _chicago_
d) blundi _Dublin_   h) arioc _cairo_

Clues

1 Ancient city in north Africa where you can visit the pyramids.
2 Densely populated city in Asia where you can eat sushi.
3 Capital of the Czech Republic.
4 Historic city and capital of Scotland.
5 World's largest capital city.
6 US city that lies on the edge of Lake Michigan.
7 Irish capital; home of James Joyce and Guinness.
8 Spain's biggest coastal city.

Grammar

1 Underline all the examples of hedging in the text below.

Are mobile phones the new cigarettes?

It has been suggested that cellular phones will be the tobacco of the 21st century. It appears that their use is almost as addictive as cigarettes, with psychologists' reports claiming that there is evidence that users display withdrawal symptoms if deprived of their mobiles for more than 24 hours. There is certainly no doubt that mobile phone use in public is just as annoying as smoking. Mobile-free zones are already being set up in cinemas and restaurants and it would seem that trains will soon be following suit with 'mobile' and 'non-mobile' carriages available on all the commuter services to London. On a more serious note, it is now widely believed that excessive mobile phone use may cause cancer, and it has been proposed that all mobile phones should carry a government health warning similar to the one displayed on cigarette packets.

2 Complete the sentences below by choosing two possible answers from the box.

> ~~appears~~ believed proof shown seem
> little ~~seems~~ recognised evidence proved
> appear hardly any

a) It _seems / appears_ that the population of many modern industrialised cities is beginning to decline.
b) There is _hardly any_ / _little_ doubt that in the future we will have to take radical action to control traffic congestion in our cities.
c) It is generally _recognised_ / _believed_ that living in cities with a population of over a million people can be detrimental to our health.
d) There is little _proof_ / _evidence_ that the levels of toxic pollution in the major cities in the U.S. are beginning to decline.
e) It would _appear_ / _seem_ that the changes in weather patterns could endanger large urban populations in low-lying land areas due to the rise in the sea level.
f) It has been _proved_ / _shown_ that prolonged exposure to the sun can cause skin cancer.

3 Rewrite these sentences using the words in the brackets.

a) Smoking can lead to cancer.
(no doubt) _There is no doubt that smoking can lead to cancer._

b) Scientists in many countries believe that increases in carbon dioxide are leading to changes in the world's climate.
(widely) _Scientists in many countries are widely active that increases in carbon dioxide are leading to changes in the world's climate._

c) There is evidence to suggest that the rate of population growth in China is beginning to decrease.
(appears) _It appears that the rate of population growth in China is beginning to decrease._

d) There is a general feeling that people believe governments are not doing enough about global warming.

(would seem) *It would seems that people believe governments are not doing enough about global warming.*

e) Scientists haven't yet produced any substantial evidence that there is life on Mars.

(there is little) *There is little evidence that however there is life on Mars.*

4 Complete the negative and limiting adverbials in the sentences below with prepositions from the box. Some of the prepositions may be used more than once.

| during   by   in   after   on   under   until |

a) The teacher told them that _____ on _____ no account were they to leave the school premises.

b) Only _____ after _____ a long wait did we finally get to hear the results of the tests.

c) We were told that _____ under _____ no circumstances were we to use our mobile phones.

d) Not even _____ in _____ summer are there so many tourists to be seen in the town.

e) Not _____ until _____ he'd left university did he really appreciate how much he'd enjoyed being a student.

f) _____ On _____ no other world capital will you find the same incredible mix of nationalities.

g) Not once _____ during _____ the whole time I knew him did he ever make a mistake in judgement.

h) Only _____ by _____ *V ing* spending a few months here will you understand how this city survives.

5 Complete the sentences with words from the box.

| barely   never   sooner   only   seldom   only after   rarely |

a) I realised how much I loved the city only _____ after _____ I had left it.

b) We had no _____ sooner _____ moved in to our new cottage than our troubles began.

c) The local people were not _____ only _____ rude to us, but they even ignored the children.

d) We had _____ never _____ *(a.)* imagined that people could be so hostile. *(a.) unfriendly & aggressive and ready to argue or fight*

e) We made our first friend _____ only _____ after two months.

f) We very _____ *rarely / seldom* _____ saw him, however, and life was still lonely.

g) The children had _____ never / rarely / seldom _____ been so quiet before.

h) We decided to go back to the city. We had _____ barely _____ put up a 'For Sale' sign when the people began to be friendly towards us!

6 Rewrite the sentences in 5 so that they begin with adverbial phrases.

a) *Only after I had left it did I realised how much I loved the city.*

b) *No sooner had we moved in to our new cottage than our troubles began.*

c) *Not only were the local people rude to us, but they even ignored the children.*

d) *Never had we imagined that people could be so hostile.*

e) *Only after two months did we made our first friend.*

f) *Rarely did we see him, however, and life was still lonely.*

g) *Never had the children been so quiet before.*

h) *We decided to go back to the city. Barely had we put up a 'For Sale' sign when the people began to be friendly towards us!*

Vocabulary

1 Match a word from column A with its opposite from column B. Then use the words from column A to complete the sentences on page 17.

A	B
a) haphazard 3	1 modest
b) tacky 5	2 unimpressive
c) clogged 4	3 organised
d) soaring 6	4 free-flowing
e) in-your-face 1	5 stylish
f) awe-inspiring 2	6 low-rise

a) I think buying plastic souvenirs on holiday is really _tacky_ .

b) With its 24-hour culture centred on gambling and entertainment, its neon signs and its brash nature, Las Vegas is one of the world's most _in-your-face_ cities.

c) Arriving in Hong Kong harbour, you're immediately struck by the _soaring_ skyscrapers that stretch as far as the eye can see.

d) The streets were _clogged_ with people waiting for the procession to start.

e) The first sight of Mount Kilimanjaro on a clear day is _awe-inspiring_ .

f) The council planned the new one-way system in a very _haphazard_ way. I kept getting lost and having to ask for directions.

2 Which is the odd one out in the following groups of words?

a) overwhelming   stunning   awe-inspiring   stylish
b) vibrant   derelict   colourful   lively
c) tacky   grubby   dirty   grimy
d) busy   bustling   energetic   dusty
e) deserted   neglected   polluted   derelict

3 Complete the texts below with these adjectives from 2.

> bustling   derelict   overwhelming   stylish
> neglected   polluted   stunning   lively

4 Find the synonyms of these definitions by solving the anagrams on the right.

a) conveniently _handily_
b) places where you can have a meal _eateries_
c) musicians who play or sing on the street _buskers_
d) to go and see what something's like _check out_
e) to watch, look at or stare at someone _gawp at_
f) to eat an enormous amount of food _gorge_
g) to complain loudly _rant_

1   kesbusr
2   hekcc tou   _check out_
3   rgoeg
4   ntar
5   pawg ta
6   yihdnal
7   etasreie

5 Use words and phrases from 4 to fill the gaps in the following text.

Covent Garden is a great place to chill out, sit back and watch the world go by. There's a whole range of different (a) _eateries_ lining the square, serving all kinds of food from all over the world. You can choose whether you want to just pick at the bar snacks served at the street cafés, or (b) _gorge_ yourself on the 'As much as you can eat for a fiver' buffet at the Taj Indian restaurant. There are always plenty of celebrities around for you to (c) _gawp at_ , and usually one or two self-proclaimed politicians (d) _ranting_ on about the state of the nation. If you prefer a spot of street theatre or a bit of music (e) _check out_ the street artists and the (f) _buskers_ . They're always guaranteed to pull a crowd.

Bangkok is an amazing sight, the sheer energy of the city is totally (a) _overwhelming_ , with its (b) _bustling_ street markets, crammed full of people from dawn to sunset, and its (c) _lively_ nightlife. In Khao San road the bars, discos and nightclubs stay open 'til the early hours of the morning. It's also a city of contrasts; hi-tech advertising standing cheek to jowl with ancient Buddhist temples, and traffic-clogged, heavily (d) _polluted_ motorways run through the middle of beautifully landscaped gardens.

Lisbon works its magic on you as soon as you arrive. Built on the hills north of the river Tagus, it looks out over (e) _stunning_ views of the estuary out towards the Atlantic Ocean. To the east of the centre lies the area of the Alfama, a fairy tale jungle of narrow streets and beautiful old houses, once (f) _neglected_ and in danger of falling into total disrepair, it is now the focus of development. The old docks, which had been (g) _derelict_ until very recently, have been renovated and are now the focus of Lisbon night life with (h) _stylish_ cafés, restaurants and clubs lining the water front, full and buzzing into the early hours.

6 Rewrite the words and phrases in *italics* in the text below with the correct form of the informal words in the box.

| nick   flog   joy-ride   boot   daft   mate |

I haven't seen my best (a) *friend* from school for years. He started (b) *stealing cars and driving them round for fun* when he was a teenager and graduated to (c) *stealing* cars which he (d) *sold* to dodgy garages in south London. He got into more and more trouble with the police. Eventually they came round to his house and raided the place. Des was so (e) *stupid*, he'd put a lot of money in biscuit tins in used notes. He even (f) *kicked* one of the policemen as they tried to arrest him. He's in prison now.

a) _mate_   d) _flogged_
b) _joy-ride_   e) _daft_
c) _nicking_   f) _booted_

Reading

1 Read these statements about the Olympics and decide if they are true (T) or false (F).

a) Originally women were not officially allowed to compete in the modern Olympics. [F]

b) The Olympic emblem with the five rings first appeared in 1913. [F]

c) Individual cities host the Olympics. [T]

d) The Olympic torch has always been part of the games. [F]

e) In the ancient games both men and woman could compete. [F]

f) Plans are underway to build a purpose built Olympic stadium. [F]

2 Now read the text and check your answers.

Every city tells a story

1   The history of the Olympic Games has always been closely related to the city that holds it. This is because it's the city, and not the country, that makes the bid to hold the Olympic Games. Understandably, the competition to hold the Olympics is fierce as it can bring great prestige and prosperity to the city.

2   From its rebirth in Athens in 1896 to the present day, the modern Olympic Games have gone through many changes. Women were not officially admitted to the Olympics until the Stockholm games of 1912, though they had participated in some events before then. In the ancient games in Greece, women were not even allowed to watch the games, let alone take part.

3   The Olympic emblem is also a relatively new addition to the game. The first emblem was designed in 1913, although the five rings weren't included until the Antwerp games of 1920. The five rings represent the union of the five continents of the world and the colours were chosen because at least one of the five colours exists in every flag of the world's nations.

4   The Olympic torch, which had been part of the ancient games, was reinstated as part of the opening ceremony in the 1928 games in Amsterdam. The idea of the torch relay (carrying a lit torch from Greece to the next Olympic venue) was introduced in the Berlin games of 1936. The relay included some 3,000

3 Complete the chart with information from the text above.

Date	City	Its story
1896	Athens	The first modern Olympic Games took place
1912	Stockholm	woman were officially admitted to the Olypices
1913		First Olympic emblem designed
1920	Antwerp	The five rings were included.
1936	Berlin	The idea of the torch relay was introduced
1992	Barcelona	Freddie Mercury and Monserrat caballé sang Olypics an which topped the charts in many countr
1496	Atlanta	Approximately 2.3 billion people watched the games on TV daily
2000	Sydney	It has the most successful Olympic games

runners who carried the torch from Greece to Germany, crossing a total of seven countries. The relay to Sydney was far more complex and involved keeping the flame alight 30,000 feet above the earth on a specially chartered transcontinental flight as well as on a short swim underwater. *(a.) crossing a continental.*

5   The Berlin games also saw the first live television transmission of the event and during the next 30 years of the Olympics there was an enormous growth in its popularity with a steady increase both in the number of sports included and the number of countries participating.

6   The 1990's also saw the massive commercialisation of the Olympics. In 1992, during the opening ceremony of the Barcelona games, Freddie Mercury and Monserrat Caballé sang an Olympic anthem which *(n.) a song which has a special important for a country it sang on special occasions.* topped the charts in many countries. The Atlanta games in 1996 had an estimated TV audience of 2.3 billion people a day and in 1995 NBC paid 1.2 billion dollars to televise the Olympic Games in Sydney. Many claim that the 2000 Olympic Games in Sydney were the most successful ever. Attendances reached record levels, with the numbers of spectators at some athletics events often exceeding 100,000.

7   The process of choosing the location for an Olympic event has become increasingly competitive over the past three decades as the rewards for staging

such an event can bring lucrative contracts and *producing a large amount of money, making a large profit* investment to the areas concerned as well as bringing a new lease of life to the city. However, it is also becoming much more difficult to host the event as the number and variety of sports grows along with the number of contestants and spectators. It has been suggested that it might be worth establishing an Olympic city, purpose built to host the games and paid for with contributions from all the participating nations. The big problem of course would be to decide where this city should be built. So at present it looks like the games will continue to travel the world, hosted by some of the world's greatest cities and bringing in their wake both glory and disruption. *make it difficult for sth. to continue in the normal way.*

---

4   Find a word in the text which means:

a)   intense (paragraph 1) *prosperity* — *(a.) very great, very strong*

b)   admiration, respect (paragraph 1) *prestige (n.)*

c)   symbol (paragraph 3) *emblem*

d)   started having (something) again (paragraph 4) *reinstated*

e)   say something that you believe is true (paragraph 6) *claim*

f)   being greater than (paragraph 6) *successful*

g)   organising (a public event) (paragraph 7) *host*

h)   very profitable (paragraph 7) *lucrative*

Pronunciation

1   🖭   Listen to this short dialogue and complete it with *just*, *really* or *actually*.

Jim: Don't you think it'd be (a) ___really___ great if Dublin could host the Olympics?

Rae: Well, I don't know, (b) ___actually___, I mean, it's a lot of hard work and all the disruption.

Jim: Do you (c) ___really___ think it wouldn't be worth it?

Rae: Well, it's (d) ___actually___ that I've been reading this book about the Olympics in Atlanta – you know, back in the nineties – now that (e) ___just___ caused a lot of problems.

Jim: Yeah, but that was different, I mean think of all the money that'd be invested in improving the city ... I think it could (f) _really_ make a real difference to people's lives.

Rae: Yeah, and for how long? (g) _just_ three weeks – it's not worth the bother.

Jim: No ... the buildings would stay, and it would (h) _actually_ put the city on the map – look what it did for Barcelona ...

🔲 Listen again and repeat using the same stress patterns as the recording.

2 Look at the short conversation. <u>Underline</u> the words the two women stress in order to add emphasis to what they're saying.

A: No, I <u>totally</u> agree. It's too much. How could they <u>possibly</u> expect you to put up with that!

B: I know, it's <u>truly</u> awful, isn't it? Such a cheek. You'd <u>honestly</u> think I was running a hotel!

A: Well, quite frankly, I think you should tell them <u>exactly</u> how you feel. That's sure to put an end to it.

🔲 Listen to the recording to check. Then repeat the conversation at the same time as the two women, taking care to use the same stress pattern.

Writing   _article_

1 Read the text below and choose the best discourse marker.

Hosting the Olympics is extremely expensive (a) _Furthermore, / However, / On the other hand,_ it can ruin the local environment. (b) _Despite / For instance, / But_ greenfields and woodlands can be lost to urban development, which means that local residents' quality of life may be diminished. (c) _In addition, / Although / On the other hand,_ it can provide a boost to the local economy, generating jobs and trade. (d) _However, / Despite / In addition,_ the effects can be all too temporary, leaving a city with unwanted installations and a huge debt to pay. (e) _Nonetheless / What's more / For example,_ with careful forward planning most of these problems can be avoided.

2 Look at the list of changes that can occur in a city when it hosts the Olympic Games.

a) Decide whether you think their effect will be a) long-term (LT) or b) short-term (ST). Write LT or ST.

b) Decide which of the changes are benefits (+) and which are drawbacks (–). Write + or – in the boxes.

1 An increase in pollution and litter _ST_ [–]
2 Improved sports installations _____ [ ]
3 More jobs in the construction industry _____ [ ]
4 Good publicity for the city _____ [ ]
5 Improved roads and airports _____ [ ]
6 More temporary accommodation facilities _____ [ ]
7 An increase in traffic congestion _____ [ ]
8 More facilities for parking cars _____ [ ]
9 Massive increase in number of visitors _____ [ ]
10 An increase in local trade _____ [ ]
11 Security problems _____ [ ]

homework

3 Your city (or a city near you) has made a bid for the Olympic Games which has been met with mixed reactions. You have been asked to write a short article for your local English language newspaper defending the bid. Your article will cover the following points:

paragraph 1: why the city would make a good venue
paragraph 2: the construction work that would be necessary
paragraph 3: the disruptions to normal lives during the games
paragraph 4: conclusion – the long and short-term benefits for the city

Make brief notes on your ideas under the four headings.

4 Look at the sentences below. Which paragraph could they be used in?

a) All in all, I think we should welcome the chance to host the games ...

b) Curiously there has been some hostility to the city's bid to host the Olympics ...

c) Although it will entail some upheaval in the short-term ...

d) However, the long-term benefits far outweigh the short-term disruption ...

e) In addition, we will need to upgrade the present infrastructure as well as ...

f) There will inevitably be some disruption to everyday lives, however ...

g) New roads will obviously be needed, as will ...

h) ... and in addition it is perfectly located ...

5 Write your article using your notes and the useful expressions from 1 and 4. You should write about 250 words.

4 Talk

homework

Famous quotes

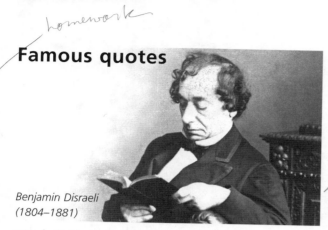

Benjamin Disraeli
(1804–1881)

Match the beginnings of the quotations in box A to their endings in box B.

A

> 4 a) There is nothing so annoying as to have two people talking
>
> 1 b) People who know little are usually great talkers,
>
> 2 c) There is one thing in the world worse than being talked about,
>
> 5 d) The guilty think all talk
>
> 6 e) The nice thing about egotists is that *a person who thinks that they are better than other people and talks too much about himself or herself*
>
> 3 f) Talk to a man about himself

B

> 1 while men who know much say little. (Jean Jacques Rousseau)
>
> 2 and that is not being talked about. (Oscar Wilde)
>
> 3 and he will listen for hours. (Benjamin Disraeli)
>
> 4 when you're busy interrupting. (Mark Twain)
>
> 5 is of themselves. (Chaucer)
>
> 6 they don't talk about other people. (Lucille S. Harper)

homework

Expressions

1 Match these expressions to their meanings.

- 3 a) to talk back to (someone)
- 6 b) to talk down to (someone)
- 4 c) to talk (someone) into (something)
- 5 d) to talk (someone) out of (something)
- 1 e) to talk over (something)
- 2 f) to talk shop

1 to discuss thoroughly
2 to discuss your work
3 to answer rudely
4 to persuade someone to do something
5 to persuade someone not to do something
6 to speak condescendingly to someone

homework — you're more important and more intelligent than other people

2 Complete these sentences with the correct form of the expressions in 1. You will need to add an object in some of the sentences.

persuade s.o. to do sth.

a) I'm sorry Paul _____*talked me into*_____ seeing that film. It was really boring.

b) Bruce and I were up late last night _____*talking over*_____ our problems, but we didn't solve anything.

c) Don't _____*talk back*_____ to me or I'll send you to bed without any supper.

d) It's so frustrating when you go out for a drink with a colleague and all they want to do is _____*talk shop*_____ = *discuss your work*

e) Oh, Anne, I'm glad I _*talked you out of*_ buying that hat. It looked ridiculous.

f) He acts like he's so important, always _*talking down to*_ everybody.

Grammar *homework*

1 There are mistakes in some of these sentences. Correct the sentences that are wrong.

a) Yesterday I'd go to the cinema with my father. *Yesterday I went to the cinema with my father.*

b) The teacher was so boring. He'd spend the first ten minutes of class calling the register and then he'd tell us to copy an exercise from the board. _____

c) Remember what Robert was like? He'll be angry for a while, then he'll forget all about it. *Remember what Robert was like? He would be angry for a while, then he would forget all about it.*

d) When he was younger he would break his leg
climbing a tree. *broke* ~~When he was younger he broke
his leg climbing a tree.~~

e) You watch. He'd come in, sit down, drink his
coffee and he wouldn't even bother to say
hello. *won't* ~~You watch. He'll come in, sit down, drink
his coffee and he won't even bother to say hello.~~

f) He was a lovely man. He would always have
time for you and he'd always ask about the
family. _____

_____

g) I've been so tired recently, I'd put something
down and forget where I've left it.
~~I've been so tired recently, I'll put
something down and forget where I've left it.~~

2 Change the present simple verbs to a form of *will*
whenever possible.

He (a) *'s* a great talker, he (b) *knows* so much
about so many different things, it (c) *'s* amazing!
And the nice thing (d) *is* he (e) *doesn't patronise*
you. He (f) *listens* carefully to your questions, no
matter how stupid and he (g) *answers* them really
patiently and he (h) *takes* time to make sure you
(i) *understand*. I think he (j) *'s* probably one of the
best teachers I've ever met.

a) _____ f) *will listen*
b) _____ g) *will answer*
c) _____ h) *will take*
d) _____ i) _____
e) *won't* j) _____

3 Change the past simple verbs and the verbs with
used to to a form of *would* whenever possible.

When we (a) *were* kids we (b) *played* football out
in the street in front of our house. I (c) *was* small
and not really very good so I (d) *was never picked*
to play and I (e) *had to* go and stand at the corner
to watch for cars coming. When a car (f) *came*
along I (g) *ran back and shouted* to the others. Then
they (h) *moved* the goals out of the way to let the
car go by. As soon as it had gone by they (i) *went*
back to their game and they (j) *forgot* all about me!
No wonder I hate football now!

a) _____ f) _____
b) *would to play* *used to* g) *would turn back and shout*
c) _____ h) *would move*
d) *never used to be picked* *would never be picked* i) *would go*
e) *would have to* *used to* j) *would forget*

4 Complete this conversation between two friends
with an appropriate form of the verb in brackets.
Use *will* or *would* whenever possible.

Jayne: Do you remember Bill? He
(a) ___*was*___ (be) a real terror in
school. Do you remember how he
(b) *would chase* (chase) the girls in the
playground, and that time when he
(c) *found* (find) an old toad and
(d) *tried* (try) to put it down the
back of your shirt?

Becky: Yes, of course I do, how could I forget!
And he (e) *would* *always get* (always / get)
his friends into trouble, he and his mates
(f) *would smoke* (smoke) behind the bike
sheds and they (g) *would always get* (always
/ get caught) *caught* by Old Robbins ...

Jayne: Yeah, and they (h) *would* *be* (be) on
detention for a week!

Becky: So what (i) *made* (make) you
bring him up in the conversation?

Jayne: Well, I (j) *bumped* (bump) into him
a couple of weeks ago down the pub and
we (k) *had* (have) a drink and
(l) *caught up* (catch up) with all the
gossip. He (m) *hasn't change* (not /
change) that much, he (n) *would still talk*
(still / talk) for hours, and he
(o) *will still tell* (still / tell) those terrible
jokes of his, but to be fair to him he
(p) *will always insist* (always / insist) on
paying for the drinks ...

Becky: 'Always' you say?

Jayne: Yeah, we've been seeing quite a lot of
each other, we (q) *will usually go* (usually /
go) to the cinema once or twice a week,
and sometimes we (r) *will have*
(have) a game of squash or tennis.

Becky: Mmm ... is it getting serious?

Jayne: I'm not sure, you can judge for yourself,
he (s) *is joining* (join) us later!

Vocabulary

1 Complete these sentences with the correct form of *conversation*.

a) I never got a chance to speak to her because she was deep in ___*conversation*___ all night

b) ___*Conversationally*___ he's totally *inept*. He never says a word. But when it comes to computer programming it's a different matter.

c) I want to improve my ___*conversational*___ French before going to Paris for the holidays.

d) They say he's a great ___*conversationalist*___. Well, I didn't think so. We sat chatting about all sorts of things and he just sat in the corner drinking brandy.

2 Put *very* or *absolutely* in the correct place in these sentences.

a) The discussion was *very* animated.

b) A: Did you like the party?
   B: Yes, I did. It was *very* enjoyable.

c) The show was *absolutely* hilarious. We haven't laughed so much for a long time.

d) His speech was *absolutely* fascinating. I never knew employment law would interest me.

e) Yes, that was a *very* memorable holiday. I wish I was still there.

f) It was *very* frustrating trying to explain the problem to him. He just wouldn't listen.

g) The discussion we had on the future of the company was *very* in-depth and we felt that we'd made some progress.

h) She thought the meeting was *absolutely* pointless. They hardly covered any of the points they planned to discuss.

i) It was a *very* lengthy conversation but in the end we did manage to come to an agreement.

3 Complete the sentences with the correct form of the words and expressions from the box.

> get a conversation going   mumble   aimlessly
> awkward silence   get a word in edgeways *(idiom) to be able to say anything because s/o else is speaking too much;*
> interrupt   never have anything to say
> hold up her end of the conversation *trying to talk* / *to remain strong and working effectively*

a) He doesn't really speak that clearly. He sort of ___*mumbles*___ the words.

b) I was really embarrassed when he asked her if she'd lost her job. There was an ___*awkward silence*___ for about ten seconds.

c) I've told you before, David. Don't ___*interrupt*___ me when I'm speaking to someone else. It's very rude.

d) They seemed to be talking about nothing in particular. They were chatting ___*aimlessly*___ about old school days.

e) She never stops talking. It's pretty difficult to ___*get a word in edgeways*___ = *trying to talk to s.o.*

f) Kevin's going through that moody teenager period. Whenever I ask him about school, he just grunts. It's really hard to ___*get a conversation going*___ *making a noise* with him.

g) She did her best to ___*hold up her end of the conversation*___ = *trying to talk*. She asked him all sorts of questions, but he asked nothing in reply.

h) She is so quiet. She ___*never have anything to say*___. She often sits there in silence throughout the whole evening.

4 Use vowels to complete the expressions so that they have the same meaning as the phrases given.

Example
He really talks a lot. You can never shut him up.
He's very *talkative*.

a) Everyone is talking about you.
   You're the t**a**lk **o**f th**e** t**o**wn.

b) It was a very short presentation.
   It was a br**ie**f t**a**lk.

c) It was a very funny presentation.
   It was a h**i**l**a**r**iou**s t**a**lk.

d) It was a very interesting presentation.
   It was a r**i**v**e**t**i**ng t**a**lk. → *very exciting*

e) A hot topic of conversation.
   The m**ai**n t**a**lk**i**ng p**oi**nt

f) To start discussions again.
   To have fr**e**sh t**a**lks.

5 Complete these sentences using your answers in 4.

Example
He's pretty quiet really. He's not the *talkative* type.

a) The unions and the management have decided that after a month of strikes they are going to sit down and begin ___*fresh talks*___.

b) They discussed all sorts of things but the _main talking point_ was the new athletic stadium and how it would be financed.

c) It was a really _riveting talk_ . He had the whole audience captivated with his stories of crossing Central Africa.

d) Well, after her fantastic appearance on the show she's become the _talk of the town_ . She's in the papers, in all the gossip columns and on the TV.

e) They had a _brief talk_ about the future of the team, but time was limited and so they plan to meet again.

f) It was a _hilarious talk_ about her failed attempts to marry a millionaire. We were all roaring with laughter in the end.

6 Match the words from column A with words from column B to make complete phrases.

A   B
5 a) all sweetness   1 rant   _(v.) to speak loudly or in a loud sound or angry voice_
4 b) caught   2 next door to
3 c) have a sit   3 down
6 d) a bite   4 my eye
1 e) shout and   5 and light
2 f) live   6 to eat

7 Rewrite the phrases in *italics* in the following sentences using the expressions in 6.

a) She was in such a bad mood the other day but now she's *so cheerful and smiley*.

_____

b) It's been a really hard day today. Let's *have a break* for five minutes.
It's been a really hard day today. Let's have a sit down for five minutes.

c) She was feeling a bit hungry so she had *a snack.*
She was feeling a bit hungry so she had a bite to eat

d) All of a sudden he lost his temper and began to *complain about this and that.*
shout and rant

e) Did you see that gold watch in the shop down the road? It really *drew my attention*. It's so unusual.
caught my eye

f) We *are neighbours* to a football-mad family.
live next door to

Pronunciation

Look at the anecdote below. You are going to listen to someone telling it. Before you do, mark where you think the speaker will pause. The first pause has been marked for you.

Sir Winston Churchill was known as being a little outspoken at times, // and he certainly didn't suffer fools gladly.//One evening//at a dinner party//he had been particularly scathing about the 'fairer sex'//when one of the women present decided she could take it no longer.//'Sir Winston,' she said,//'If I were your wife, I'd put poison in your tea!'.//Without stopping to take breath, the great man turned to her and said.//'My dear lady, if I were your husband, I'd drink it.'

Listen to check your answers.

Listen again and mark the main stresses. Then repeat the anecdote in time with the speaker.

Listening & reading

1 A shaggy dog story is a long-winded _(n.) a very long joke with a silly or disappointing ending_ anecdote whose sole purpose is to build up to a _(n.) the last few words of a that make it funny_ punchline. Cover the tapescript, listen to this shaggy dog story and choose the correct punchline.

a) … we've got a good selection of ties.

b) … we can't let you in without a tie.

c) … we haven't got any water.

d) … we're closed right now.

Have you heard the one about the man in the desert? _(n.) the speed at which sth. walks, runs or moves_

1 There's this man who wins a jeep in a competition and decides he wants to put it through its paces. So he plans a five day trip in the desert. The first couple of days the jeep's performing fine and the man's _(idiom) to have a very good time_ having a whale of a time, charging up and down dunes, chasing along old river beds and even happening across a couple of _a small hilly pond formed by river_ oases. But on the third day he runs into trouble. The jeep breaks down in the middle of nowhere and he's forced to abandon it and set off on foot. He takes a couple of water bottles with him and sets off towards the nearest village.

2 He walks all day and all night with no sign of the village. His water is starting to run low but he keeps going. He knows he'll get there sooner or later. However, another day and another night pass by and his water has run out totally. By now he's forgotten all about rescuing his jeep, or even about getting to the village. His only thought now is to find water or he'll die of thirst.

[handwritten top margin, annotation next to "nomad":] (n) a number of tribe that moves from its animals from place to place

3   In the distance he sees the figure of a (nomad) walking towards him across the desert. To start with he can't believe his eyes, he thinks it must be a (mirage), but no, the nomad comes closer and closer and finally appears there in front of him. He greets the nomad and asks him if he has any water to sell him. The nomad apologises, explaining that he's just finished the last of his water but offers to sell him a tie. The man finds it hard not to laugh in his face, why should he want a tie in the desert? He refuses the offer very politely and asks the nomad for directions to the nearest village. They part and go their separate ways.

[handwritten annotation near "mirage":] (n) an effect caused by hot air in deserts or on roads, that make you think you can see water, which is not there.

4   A few hours later the man sees a small group of women sitting by the side of the road. He asks them for water, but curiously their answer is the same as the nomad's; they have no water, but they do have a wide selection of ties. The man walks on, beginning to fear for his sanity. As he climbs over the top of a dune, he spies a tent. He walks towards it as quickly as his tired legs can take him. His only thought is water. But the answer he receives is the same as before. (Exasperated,) he wanders on, having almost given up all hope.

[handwritten annotation near "Exasperated":] (v.) to annoy or irritate sb very much

5   He's on his last legs when he sees a hotel on the horizon. It glimmers in the heat of the sun. It must surely be a mirage. But no, as he drags himself painfully towards the main entrance, he sees that it's real. He has finally reached civilisation. His nightmare is over. He can (quench his thirst,) hire a car, rescue his jeep and set off back home. With his last ounce of strength he straightens up, walks up the stairs to the front door, and asks the doorman for a drink of water. The doorman shakes his head sadly and says, 'I'm sorry sir, but ...'

2   [cassette icon]   Listen to the story again or read the tapescript and answer these questions.

a)   Why was the man in the desert?
Because he wanted to try his new jeep.

b)   How long has the man been in the desert when he meets the nomad?
It was two days and two nights.

c)   How many times does he ask for water?
Three times + fourth times

d)   Why does he think the hotel is a mirage?
Because it was glimmers in the heat of the sun when he see it.

e)   Does he eventually get a drink of water?
No he doesn't. +

3   Match the two halves of the phrases. Then check your answers with the text.

A

3 a)   put it through
5 b)   having
1 c)   a wide
2 d)   quench
7 e)   set off
6 f)   run
8 g)   fear for
4 h)   on

B

1   selection
2   his thirst
3   its paces
4   his last legs
5   a whale of a time
6   low
7   on foot
8   his sanity

4   Match each phrase in 3 to its definition below.

1   be worried that he is going mad   *8 (g)*
2   try something out to see how well it performs   *3(a)*
3   stop him feeling thirsty   *2 (d)*
4   start walking   *7 (e)*
5   coming to the end of a supply of something   *6(f)*
6   really enjoying himself   *5 (b)*
7   a lot of things to choose from   *1 (c)*
8   be about to collapse   *4 (h)*

5   Complete these sentences with some of the expressions in 3. Make any necessary changes.

a)   I hadn't played for ages. I was practically _on my last legs_ by the end of the match.

b)   The kids were running around, shouting and playing and _having a whale of a time._

c)   The new coach really _put_ the team _through its paces_ in his first training session.

d)   The class had been misbehaving all day and the teacher's patience was beginning to _run low_.

e)   Tell John to try some of this lemon juice. It'll really _quench his thirst_.

Writing

1 You are going to write a shaggy dog story about a librarian. Before you do so, look back at the story about the man in the desert and answer the following questions:

a) What tense is used throughout? _present simple_

b) What is the main topic of each paragraph? Match the paragraph with the summaries below:

   1   the first attempt to buy water `3`

   2   building up the drama of the situation `2`

   3   the climax of the story as the man comes across the hotel `5`

   4   subsequent attempts to buy water `4`

   5   an explanation of why he was stuck in the desert `1`

c) Find three examples of inflated or dramatic language which add to the build up of the story.

   Example
   Exasperated, he wanders on …

2 Look at the cartoon below and complete the punchline.

Have you heard the one about the librarian and the chicken?

a)

b)

c)

d)

e)

The chicken puts the book down at the frog's feet and the frog says, '_____'.

3 Here are the topics for the five main paragraphs of the story. Put them in order.

a) The repeated daily visits and the librarian's suspicions `d` _b_

b) An introduction to the librarian `b` _a_

c) The librarian follows the chicken and unveils the solution to the mystery `e` _d_

d) The chicken's second visit `c` _c_

e) The first time the chicken visits the library `a` _e_

4 Write the full story of the librarian and the chicken. Remember to build up slowly to the climax.

5 Luck

Superstitions

Complete these sentences about superstitions in the UK using the words in the box.

> your left hand   a falling leaf   a rabbit's foot
> a mirror   a ladder   a black cat

a) If you break ___a mirror___ , you'll have seven years' bad luck.

b) Keeping ___a rabbit's foot___ in your pocket will bring you good luck.

c) Don't walk under ___a ladder___ as you're bound to have an accident.

d) Catch ___a falling leaf___ in your hand and you'll avoid a cold the following season.

e) If ___a black cat___ crosses your path, you'll have some good luck.

f) If ___your left hand___ itches, you're about to come into some money.

Grammar

1 Read the text about the Gorden family. Then use the prompts below to write unreal conditional sentences using *if*.

Example
if / house flooded / not / get builders in
If the house hadn't been flooded, they wouldn't have got builders in.

a) builders / not knock wall down / if not absolutely necessary

_____

b) if / not knock down wall / not discover secret room

_____

c) if / not discover secret room / sketches / never found

_____

d) sketches / be on display / museum / if builders / not find

_____

e) if / not rain so heavily / they / now live another house

_____

Lucky discovery gives the Gordens three extra rooms

Returning home from a trip abroad, Brian and Jenny Gorden were horrified to find their 17th century cottage under two metres of water, following the recent floods. The cottage was so severely damaged that they had to call the builders in. While knocking down a section of the wall, the builders were amazed to discover a 'secret room'. In it they found a collection of original sketches by a famous local artist, several pieces of antique furniture, an impressive collection of antique dolls and a dolls house. They also came across the original deeds to the house, revealing another two hidden rooms. Brian Gorden remarked, 'We're absolutely gobsmacked. We were thinking of buying a bigger house but now we've got three more rooms.' The builders have started to renovate the rooms and the sketches and dolls have been given to the local museum.

2 Complete the beginning of these unreal conditionals and each of their three endings. Use the verb in brackets in the appropriate form.

a) If I _____ (not / stand) behind the door,

  1 I _____ (not / hear) what they were saying.

  2 it _____ (not / hit) me in the face.

  3 I _____ (not / have) a broken nose!

b) If I _____ (not do) the entry exam tomorrow,

  1 I _____ (go) away last weekend.

  2 I _____ (come) to the party tonight.

  3 I _____ (be) in a much better mood!

c) If she _____ (ask) his boss a little sooner,

  1 she _____ (be) very happy to help him.

  2 he _____ (not / be) in this mess now.

  3 he _____ (go) on holiday with the rest of us next week.

3 Look at these sentences using *wish / if only*. Five of the sentences contain a mistake. Correct the mistakes.

a) Congratulations. I wished you all the happiness in the world.

b) If only I was concentrating when we did the exercise yesterday.

c) I wish I could spend more time at home with the kids.

d) If only she listened to what he said, she wouldn't be in the predicament she's in now.

e) I wish I am not going to New York tomorrow. I hate flying.

f) I wish you wouldn't keep tapping your foot like that. It's driving me mad.

g) I wish informed you that your membership has expired.

h) If only you could see me now.

4 What would you say? Write a wish or a regret using the words given.

a) I don't have a lot of free time at the moment.

  I wish _____

b) I didn't go to bed 'til very late last night and now I'm really tired.

  I wish / earlier _____

  _____

c) It would be nice to be able to take some time off work to go on holiday, but it just isn't possible.

  If only _____

  _____

d) I said I'd go to the party and now I don't want to go at all.

  I regret _____

  _____

e) I missed the train because I wasn't listening to the announcements!

  I wish _____

  _____

f) I really should have revised more for the exam.

  I regret _____

  _____

g) I left home so late that I missed the plane.

  If only / late _____

  _____

h) I have some bad news for you, I'm afraid you've failed all your exams.

  I regret _____

  _____

5 Circle the most appropriate verb form in the texts below.

It's no good now saying I wish I (a) *bought / 'd bought* one. I didn't and that's that. But it's really annoying to think that the one week I didn't buy a lottery ticket my lucky numbers came up. Oh, if only I (b) *'d stopped / stopped* at the shop to buy one, but on Friday I was in such a rush that I forgot. You know, if I'd won I could (c) *lie / be lying* on the beach somewhere now (d) *drink / drinking* a tropical fruit cocktail.

I wish you (e) *told / 'd told* me that you were coming to Naples, we (f) *'d have / could have* met up. I (g) *might have / 'd have* taken you to the restaurant down the road – it's great. The food is excellent and you (h) *could have / should have* tried some of our local dishes.

I wish I (i) *could play / could have played* tennis better, but I never seem to have enough time to practise. If only I (j) *didn't have to / hadn't had to* work so much. I rarely get home from work before nine in the evening.

Vocabulary

1 Read the newspaper story below about a lucky lottery winner. The text assumes a lot of knowledge of British popular culture. How much do you know? Do the quiz and see.

Fortunate Fiona wins big Roll-Over in Mail's Saturday Lottery

Fiona couldn't believe her eyes when she saw the numbers on the front page of *The Mail* in her local Co-op. She dashed off home to check her ticket and then, grabbing her mac and umbrella, set off for a swift one in her local to celebrate the big win. The barmaid, on seeing her excited face, asked her if she'd just won the lottery. Fiona beamed, admitted that she had and bought a round of champagne for everyone in the bar. She's currently sunning herself on the deck of a liner on a once-in-a-lifetime cruise around the Med.

---

a A 'roll-over' is …
1 a kind of sports competition
2 winnings that have accumulated over two weeks or more
3 a vintage car

b 'The Mail' is …
1 a letter that has just arrived in the post
2 an e-mail provider
3 a daily newspaper

c The 'Co-op' is …
1 a supermarket
2 a school
3 a bus stop

d A 'mac' is …
1 a laptop computer
2 a raincoat
3 a breed of dog

e 'A swift one' is …
1 a very fast runner
2 a quick telephone call
3 a quick drink

f A 'local' is …
1 a pub near her house
2 her neighbour's house
3 the shopping centre

g A 'round of champagne' is …
1 a barrel of champagne
2 a bottle of champagne
3 a glass of champagne for everyone present

h 'Med' is …
1 some medicine
2 the Mediterranean sea
3 a medium sized boat

---

2 Replace the words in *italics* in the sentences with words from the box.

> peered   clenched   scrabbled about
> tailed off   slipped off   flitted

a) He couldn't believe the news. He walked away from the group and *left quietly* without saying anything to anybody.   *slipped off*

b) I don't think I've ever been so scared. I shut my eyes and *tightly closed* my fist.   *clenched*

c) It was a chance to catch up with all her old school friends and she *moved around* from table to table talking to everyone.   *flitted*

d) Suddenly all his change fell on the floor and everyone *rushed around*, picking it up for him.   *scrabbled about*

e) As they walked off into the distance their voices *died down*.   *tailed off*

f) I *looked* over the high fence to see if I could see anyone but nobody seemed to be at home.   *peered*

3 Complete the text below with phrases from the box.

> wishing well   Wishing you all the best
> Best wishes   wishful thinking   make a wish
> grant three wishes   have your wish come true

Wish Fulfilment

According to superstition there are lots of occasions when you can
(a) _make a wish_ . For example, when you blow out all the candles on your birthday cake, or if you can catch a falling leaf in autumn. However, whatever the reason for making a wish, secrecy is of utmost importance if you want to (b) _have your wish come true_ , so remember, never tell anyone what you wished for, no matter how much they insist!

Another tradition associated with wishes is that of the (c) _wishing well_ , often found in the main square of a small town. If you throw a coin into it you can make a wish. And of course many traditional fairy tales are built around a mystical figure who can
(d) _grant three wishes_ , such as the fairy godmother in Cinderella or the Genie in the Lamp.

Even in everyday speech wishes can still be very important. We often sign off letters to friends and family with the words (e) '_Best wishes_

_____ ' and send greetings cards which read (f) '~~wishing you all the best~~_____ in your new home / new job / retirement'. And of course, most of us indulge in (g) ~~wishful~~_____ ~~thinking~~ at times, losing ourselves in impossible daydreams about wonderful plans and achievements.

[handwritten annotations: "to allow yourself to have or do sth. that you like"]

Listening

1   ▭ Listen to two friends talking about a film and decide if the following statements are true (T) or false (F).

a)   They both watched the film last night. ☐

b)   The film is a comedy. ☐

c)   The story is very simple. ☐

d)   It has a happy ending. ☐

e)   It's not really worth seeing. ☐

2   ▭ Read the summary of the film. Listen again and complete the summary.

Inspired by a true story, (a) _____ is a hilarious comedy about everyone's dream – (b) _____ . Set in (c) _____ , in the tiny coastal village of Tulaigh Morh, it is the comic tale of Jackie O'Shea (Ian Bannen) and Michael O'Sullivan (David Kelly) and a (d) _____ that changes the lives of the community forever.

When one day Jackie discovers that someone from his own village has (e) _____ , he suggests to his life-long friend Michael O'Sullivan that they should (f) _____ , befriend them and share in the (g) _____ . After a series of false leads they eventually find the winner.

Ned Devine is (h) _____ in his bed with the (i) _____ in his hand and a fixed smile on his face. After playing (j) _____ , he wins, only to die from (k) _____ . Ned has no family and (l) _____ , so Jackie decides that Michael should (m) _____ and try to get the winnings.

Nervous that things are getting out of hand, Michael tries to talk Jackie out of it. But when the (n) _____ arrives unexpectedly from Dublin to (o) _____ there's no turning back. Eventually, Jackie and Michael realise that they have to involve the whole village in the (p) _____ if they are to succeed. The events that unfold are more dramatic than winning the lottery itself.

3   Complete the extracts from the recording by combining a verb in an appropriate form from box A with a preposition from box B.

A

| dress   track   hand   turn   work   come   set   keel |

B

| over   up   over   in   up   down   up   out |

a)   … this story is _____ a tiny old village near the sea in the Republic of Ireland.

b)   … they decide to _____ the winner, befriend him or her, whoever they are …

c)   … when he actually does win he _____ and dies from the shock of it!

d)   … when the Lottery representative _____ from Dublin to check the claim …

e)   … there's this hilarious scene where Michael has to _____ as Ned …

f)   But of course everything _____ all right in the end.

g)   … persuade the Lottery representative to _____ the money …

h)   … this superb scene of a group of the men from the village standing on the cliff top watching the sun _____ and drinking a last toast to the memory of Ned Devine.

▭ Listen to check your answers. (Or look at the tapescript on page 78.)

Writing

1 Read the review of the film given below. Which of the following things does it mention?

  a) the main plot ☐

  b) the location ☐

  c) the soundtrack ☐

  d) the quality of the acting ☐

  e) the director ☐

  f) a particularly memorable scene ☐

  g) the camerawork ☐

  h) the author's personal response to the film ☐

  i) a personal recommendation ☐

  j) the sub-plots ☐

2 Find words in the text which mean:

  a) extremely funny (paragraph 2)

    _____

  b) rhythm or speed (paragraph 2)

    _____

  c) very talented (paragraph 2) _____

  d) stories which unfold at the same time as the main story (paragraph 5) _____

  e) not obvious (paragraph 6) _____

  f) an unexpected element at the end of a story (paragraph 6) _____

3 Match the following summaries to the seven paragraphs in the review.

  a) The first sub-plot ☐

  b) A brief summary of the premise of the film ☐

  c) A particularly funny scene ☐

  d) A list of its main qualities ☐

  e) The second sub-plot ☐

  f) A catchy description of the film and a personal recommendation ☐

  g) A brief description of the main plot ☐

4 You are going to write a review of a film you have really enjoyed. Decide which film you are going to write about. Then look at the list in 1 and decide which points you are going to include. Use the review of *Waking Ned* as a model.

12/09/1998

Movie Review | Film | Video | TV | Radio

Movie Review by Heather Clisby

1 Someone in the tiny town of Tulaigh Morh, population 52, has won Ireland's seven-million-pound national lottery but the question is who?

2 Such is the premise for *Waking Ned*, a hilarious film that lightly explores the prospects of sudden wealth. Shot on the breathtakingly beautiful Isle of Man, this charming film is blessed with a swift pace, a strong story, gifted actors and a strict focus. (Are you listening, Hollywood?)

3 The first half of the film is a process of elimination as Jackie, Annie and their best pal, Michael, played by the very game David Kelly, go about deducing who the lucky winner might be. Just to be sure that their position is clear, they become the most generous and loving pals to every town member suspected of being a closet millionaire. After buying a few pints and throwing dinner parties, they bring suspicion upon themselves.

4 In the cinematic realm, there exist rare scenes that are instant classics. In *Waking Ned* there is such a scene and it includes an old motorcycle and one very flustered and very naked elderly gentleman. The audience was literally screaming with hysterical laughter, myself included. Bravo, David Kelly, for really giving us your . . . everything.

5 There are two charming sub-plots in the film that play nicely with one another. In one, two men vie for the hand of a beautiful single mother, Maggie. The first is a shallow ladies man and the other is an honest pig farmer. She loves the farmer but can't quite get past the smell, despite his efforts with fruity soaps.

6 Then there is the nine-year-old boy, Maggie's son, who strikes up a philosophical friendship with the young priest filling in for the village's vacationing clergyman. In a beautiful and subtle twist, the boy emerges as the wise guide to the holy man's naive sufferings. In the final scene, we learn more about the boy's background and then it all makes complete divine sense.

7 The best thing about *Waking Ned* is that one can't decide what the best thing is. Clever and unpredictable, funny and endearing, level and unpreachy, *Waking Ned* is a joy.

© Heather Clisby

6 *Mind*

homework

Mind songs

the words of a song

1 Complete the song lyrics by matching a phrase from box A with a phrase from box B.

A

2

4

3

1

a)	Little things I should have said and done, I just never took the time ...
b)	Why can't you see what you're doing to me when you don't believe a word I'm saying ...
c)	Cause I've made my mind up,
d)	If you change your mind, I'm first in line ...

B

1	... honey, I'm still free, take a chance on me (ABBA: *Take a Chance On Me*)
2	... you were always on my mind, you were always on my mind (Elvis Presley: *Always On My Mind*)
3	... you're going to be mine (Donovan: *Sunshine Superman*)
4	... we can't go on together with suspicious minds, we can't build our dreams with suspicious minds (Elvis Presley: *Suspicious Minds*)

2 Complete the following sentences using the expressions with *mind* from the song lyrics.

a) They really don't trust anything anybody tells them. They've got very *suspicious minds*.

b) Sorry, I wasn't paying attention, I've got something *on my mind*.

c) Listen, I know you've decided you don't want to go, but if you *change your mind* the invitation's still open.

d) I've finally *made my mind up*. I'm going to quit my job and travel around the world!

homework

Grammar

1 Some of these sentences have mistakes in them. Correct the ones that are wrong.

feel (stative)

a) What do you fancy doing? I'm feeling like going to the cinema.

b) I'm feeling a bit ill at the moment. I think it must be the change in the weather.

c) She didn't know what the homework was because she wasn't hearing what the teacher was saying. *listening to (dynamic)*

heard

d) He was hearing strange noises coming from the cellar, so he grabbed a torch and climbed down to investigate.

e) I've been hearing quite a lot from Dave recently. He e-mails me almost every day.

can smell

f) I think I'm smelling something burning. Are you sure you switched the cooker off?

g) A: What are you doing?
   B: I'm just tasting the sauce. I think it needs more cheese.

tastes

h) This fish is tasting funny. Are you sure it's OK to eat?

2 Circle the correct verb form.

stative

a) I'm hearing / (can hear) a noise outside. Can you see if it's the cat? *stative*

b) She *couldn't taste* / *didn't taste* the salt so she decided to add a bit more.

c) I *can smell* / (*am smelling*) the milk to see if it is fresh. *dynamic*

d) He wasn't really *hearing* / (*able to hear*) the song that clearly because of the noise in the background. *stative*

e) As soon as they walked in the room they (*could smell*) / *were smelling* gas.

stative

homework

3 Rewrite the sentences using a participle clause.

Example

He hadn't really understood what she'd said so he did the exercise incorrectly.

Not having understood what she said, he did the exercise incorrectly.

He's English so he finds it hard to follow them when they start speaking Czech.

Being English he finds it hard to follow them when they start speaking Czech.

a) We worked really hard at the meeting, so we all went for a meal on the company.

Having worked really hard at the meeting, we all went for a meal on the company.

b) He doesn't know the area very well so there's a danger he'll get lost.

Not knowing the area very well so there's a danger he will get lost.

c) He was cleared of theft by the courts and immediately got his old job back.

Having been cleared of theft by the courts and immediately got his old job back.

d) He was lost in thought and didn't notice that his train had pulled out of his station.

Being lost in thought and didn't notice that his train had pulled out of his station.

e) She didn't make a very good impression at the interview and was worried that she wouldn't get the job.

Not having made a very good impression at the interview and was worried that she wouldn't get the job.

f) She wasn't particularly interested in the talk and decided not to go.

Not being particularly interested in the talk and decided not to go.

g) James was delayed by the traffic on the motorway so he was extremely late.

Having been delayed by the traffic on the motorway so James was extremely late.

h) He was intrigued by the news and wanted to know more.

Being intrigued by the news, he wanted to know more.

4 Read the text below and circle the most appropriate participle clause.

Pushy passengers win airline dispute

Fifty-four economy class passengers, (a) *spending / having spent / spent* three hours waiting at Heathrow airport, were finally informed that their flight had been cancelled due to technical problems. On (b) *hearing / having heard / heard* the news, one of the older passengers marched up to the airline offices, (c) *demanding / having demanded / demanded* that they all be put on the next possible flight. However, (d) *overbooking / having overbooked / overbooked* the next flight, there was very little the airline could do.

The passengers all crowded around the airline desk, (e) *shouting and protesting / having shouted and protested / shouted and protested*. (f) *Wanted / Having wanted / Wanting* to do something to appease the angry crowd, they finally offered all the passengers free flights to the destination of their choice. (g) *Appeasing / Having appeased / Appeased* by this offer, they calmed down, took their seats and waited another three hours before they finally took off, more than six hours late.

anger was reduced & satisfied what they been on.

Vocabulary

1 Look at the anagrams. Rearrange the letters to make verbs associated with seeing.

a) zega — *gaze* = to look steadily at sth (v.) + adv/prep for a long time

b) menixae — *examine*

c) conrigese — *recognise*

d) ratd — *dart* = to look at sth suddenly and quickly (v.t)

e) ecveipre — *perceive* = to notice or become aware of sth.

f) cnas — *scan*

2 Replace a word in these sentences with *observe*, *see* or *recognise*.

a) I admit that it's not an easy language to learn.
recognise
I recognise that it is not an easy language to learn.

b) He doesn't really understand what you are trying to say.
see
He doesn't really see what you are trying to say.

c) They spent most of the day watching the house but nothing unusual happened.
observing
They spent most of the day observing the house but nothing unusual happened.

d) They have finally acknowledged his effort in the peacekeeping process.

recognised

They have finally recognised his effort in the peacekeeping process.

e) 'What a ridiculous attitude to take towards your studies,' remarked the teacher.

observed

What a ridiculous attitude to take towards your studies; observed the teacher

f) She said she was thinking of meeting Massimo later that evening.

seeing

She said she was thinking of seeing Massimo later that evening

g) My advice to you is to obey the law. If you don't, you'll be in trouble.

observe

My advice to you is to observe the law. If you don't, you'll be in trouble.

h) As soon as I saw him, I thought I knew him.

As soon as I saw him I thought I recognised

3 Circle the correct word in the sentences below.

a) The doctor gazed / (examined) / perceived the X-ray very carefully before speaking.

b) He panicked, his eyes (darting) / gazing / scanning from side to side, looking for a way out.

c) It really depends on how you examine / (perceive) / scan change. Some people really enjoy it, other people really worry about it.

d) He looked at me for a long time and then shook his head. He really didn't seem to scan / examine / (recognise) me.

e) He (scanned) / darted / recognised the newspaper, looking for the article they'd just mentioned.

f) She examined / (gazed) / perceived out of the window at the pouring rain, thinking of anything but the lesson going on around her.

4 Complete these sentences with words from the box.

| rumour   nap   docile   tattered   phobia |
| addiction |

a) There's a ___rumour___ going round that Pete's having an affair with Jenny.

b) I've got a ___phobia___ about cockroaches. I can't stand the sight of them.

c) You look tired. Why don't you have a ___nap___ for twenty minutes.

d) Sam's dog is very ___docile___. He sleeps all day and lets the children climb all over him.

e) With Michaela's ___addiction___ to chocolate it's no wonder she's putting on weight.

f) What have you done to that book? Look at the state of it. It's all ___tattered___.

5 Complete these expressions with *mind* with words from the box.

| come   up   speak   in   never   do   two |
| how |

a) Mind ___how___ you go.

b) Something will ___come___ to mind.

c) I'm in ___two___ minds.

d) ___Never___ mind.

e) Bear it ___in___ mind.

f) ___Do___ you mind?

g) Make ___up___ your mind.

h) ___Speak___ your mind.

6 Complete these sentences with expressions in 5. Make any changes that are necessary.

a) Come on. We really have to make a decision now. You're going to have to ___make up your mind___.

b) It's not a major point but if I were you, I'd ___bear it in mind___. It's worth considering.

c) I hope ___something will come to mind___. I really can't think of anything at the moment and we need some ideas before the meeting tomorrow.

d) I wish you'd be more decisive. You're constantly ___in two minds___. One minute you say one thing and the next minute you say the opposite.

e) ___Mind how you go___. It's been snowing all night and the roads will be icy.

f) He always says exactly what he thinks and I admire people who ___speak their minds___.

g) ___Do you mind___ if I smoke at the table or would you prefer me to go outside?

h) ___Never mind___. There'll always be other opportunities in the future.

Listening

1 📼 Listen to Mark, Kay and Liz talking about stress. (If you don't have the recording, read the tapescript on page 79.) Make notes on the following questions:

a) What is the cause of their stress?

Mark: _____

_____

Kay: _____

_____

Liz: _____

_____

b) How does it affect them?

Mark: _____
_____

Kay: _____
_____

Liz: _____
_____

c) What do they do to counter it?

Mark: _____
_____

Kay: _____
_____

Liz: _____
_____

2 Which of the three people, Mark, Kay or Liz:

a) feels the need to do something intellectually challenging?

b) doesn't like spending free time talking about work?

c) finds that noise can be a source of stress?

d) suffers from the physical effects of stress?

e) suffers from the emotional effects of stress?

f) combats stress with physical activities?

g) combats stress with social activities?

h) combats stress with domestic activities?

3 Turn to the tapescript on page 79 and find words or phrases that mean:

a) to relax (Mark) _____

b) unable to sit still because they're nervous or bored (Mark) _____

c) escape (Mark) _____

d) held back, shut in (Mark) _____

e) so boring it makes you depressed (Kay) _____

f) without energy (Kay) _____

g) to lie or sit with knees pulled up so as to make yourself comfortable (Kay) _____

h) becoming useless (Liz) _____

4 Use some of the words and phrases in 3 to complete the following short text. Make any necessary changes.

If you want to combat stress it's very important to find a way to release (a) _____ energy or you'll find that you can't

(b) _____ properly and this often means that when it comes to going to bed you're still (c) _____ and will find it very difficult to get to sleep.

If you often come home from work feeling (d) _____ and exhausted, try and create some kind of routine that helps you (e) _____ all the stresses and strains of your job. Some people like to do sport, others like to go out with friends, whilst some may prefer to (f) _____ with a hot cup of chocolate in front of the television.

Writing

~~homework~~

1 A friend of yours wrote you the following letter. She's obviously under a lot of stress. Read the letter and answer the following questions.

a) What is the cause of her stress?

_____

b) What effect is it having on her?

_____

c) What advice did her boyfriend give her?

_____

Hi, how are things with you?

I'm feeling pretty miserable, actually, I hope you don't mind me writing to you just to get things off my chest. I've got a terrible cold which really isn't helping me study, and makes me feel really tired. But still no matter how tired I am, I just can't sleep!

As you know, I've got my final exams looming at the end of next month and I'm getting massively stressed out over them. I'm studying twelve or more hours a day without stopping, no time to do any sport, not even enough time to go shopping! I'm living on junk food and coffee — not healthy I know, but what can I do? I really have to pass these exams. And I'm getting really touchy too. I had a really bad argument with Tom yesterday. He was telling me I should take it easy, get out a bit, unwind, that it'd do me good. I know he means well, but he isn't studying, he just doesn't understand. Anyway, I really snapped at him and he just walked out. I haven't seen him since. It feels like this'll never end sometimes — tell me there's a life waiting for me after all this!! I honestly can't take much more.

Anyway, back to work ... again! See you soon, once all this is over. not see her then

2002

All the best,
Jane.

2 Which of the following points would you include in a reply to Jane's letter? Choose the best five or six. Be comforting without sounding too pushy. Is there anything else you would like to add?

a) She must try to eat properly, it'll give her more energy.

b) Doing sport really helps boost energy levels and clear the mind.

c) Seeing people, even if it's just for half an hour over a coffee, is really important to stop her from getting depressed and touchy.

d) Studying in short bursts and taking short breaks is far more efficient than slogging away for hours on end. *hard working*

take your mind off thing could help.

may be e) She could try watching TV for half an hour before going to bed.

① call him , apologize

f) She should listen to her boyfriend.

g) A glass of hot milk is really good to help you sleep. *hot chocolate*

h) She's a good student and has never failed an exam in her life, why should she fail now?

i) You were in the same position last year so you understand exactly how she feels. *went out*

may be j) Offer to cook for her for a week.

k) Promise her a wonderful weekend away after the exams have finished.

may be l) Ask her to phone you sometime, it can really help to talk things through.

3 Here's a letter Steve sent to Fran when she was feeling a bit low. Look at the three main paragraphs. In which paragraph does he:

a) make a funny remark to lighten the tone? [3]

b) respond directly to what Fran said in her last letter? [1]

c) let her know he believes in her ability to cope with the situation? [3]

d) offer some concrete advice as to how to improve the situation? [2]

e) warn her about the consequences for her health? [1]

f) offer sympathy and understanding? [1]

g) offer to do something to help? [3]

Dearest Fran,

1 How are you? You sounded really low in your last letter. It made me feel quite worried for you. Are things getting any better? Were you serious about resigning or were you just going through a bad patch? Look, if the job's really that bad, I think you should give it up. Nothing's worth getting that stressed out about. But if you're really determined to stick it out, and I know you, you can be really stubborn sometimes, you should really try looking after yourself a bit better. I'm sure you can find ways to delegate some of your work or to cut down on your workload. They really are asking too much of you.

2 I think the best thing you could do would be to sit down with your boss and talk about the situation. Maybe she doesn't realise the pressure you're under. Or maybe you should ask for a short holiday before you literally work yourself into the ground. You can't keep working the way you have been, it'll make you ill.

3 Right, sorry, I sound like your mother! But seriously, if there's anything I can do, please let me know. And remember, nothing lasts for ever. Whatever you decide to do, I'm sure you'll make the right decision and it'll all work out fine in the long run. In the meantime, phone me. I'd love to hear from you and maybe we can make some plans to meet up. So take care and don't let it get you down. A huge hug and lots of love,
Steve

4 Make a note of any useful language you would like to use in your letter to Jane.

5 Now write your letter to Jane. You should write between 200 and 250 words.

7 Review 1

Grammar

1 Correct the mistakes in these sentences.

cond. a) I wish I ~~was~~ [had been] listening when he gave out the instructions.

I wish I had been listening when he gave out the instructions

adding emphasis b) I thought the show was very hilarious.

I thought the show was ~~very~~ really hilarious

with + regret c) I regret informing you that your application has been rejected.

I regret to inform you that your application has been rejected.

cond. d) If I'd known that she was going to be there last night, I might ~~go~~ to the party.

If I'd known that she was going to be there last night, I might have gone to the party.

sense (stative v.) e) Call the gas board. I'm smelling gas.

Call the gas board. I can smell gas

limiting adv. broad f) Never, I have heard such a ridiculous excuse.

Never have I've heard such a ridiculous excuse.

past participle g) Not really understood, I asked her to repeat the instructions.

Not really having understood, I asked her to repeat the instructions.

situations specific h) We would stay up all night talking things through last weekend.

We stayed up all night talking things through last weekend.

describing nouns i) That quaint ~~fish little~~ restaurant that your mother likes has closed down.

That quaint little fish restaurant that your mother likes has closed down.

phrasal v. j) She looked ~~the essay through~~ very carefully before handing it in.

She looked through the essay very carefully before handing it in.

2 Rewrite these sentences using the key words in brackets.

cond. a) I really regret not accepting that job.
(If only) *If only I had accepted the job.*

past part. b) Once I'd heard his side of the argument I decided to go along with the idea.
(Having) *Having heard his side of the argument I decided to go along with the idea.*

cond. c) She didn't buy the dress because there was a small stain on the arm.
(if) *She would have bought the dress if there hadn't been a small stain on the arm.*

tendencies d) When we were younger, we used to go camping at the weekends.
(would) *When we were younger, we would go camping at the weekends.*

wish + regret e) If only I'd more time to spend on my studies.
(wish) *I wish I had more time to spend on my studies.*

tendencies f) He comes in, sits down and doesn't say a word to anyone.
(will) *He'll come in, sits down and won't say a word to anyone.*

past part. g) The sound woke him and he immediately went downstairs to investigate.
(Woken by) *Woken by the sound, he immediately went downstairs to investigate.*

cont. h) She can't sleep because she drank a strong cup of coffee before going to bed.
(If) *If she hadn't drunk a strong cup of coffee before going to bed she'd be able to sleep.*

wish + regret i) We would like to take this opportunity to congratulate you on your recent promotion.
(wish) *We wish to take this opportunity to congratulate you on your recent promotion.*

limiting adv. broad j) I can't remember seeing him ever actually helping anyone or doing anything nice.
(Not once) *Not once can I remember seeing him ever actually helping anyone or doing anything nice.*

3 Circle the correct word or phrase in the text below.

A London based newspaper recently decided to test security in various key 'Hot Spots' around England. In the first of a series of tests a journalist, (a) *hiring / having hired* a pilot's uniform from a fancy dress shop, and after (b) *reproducing / reproduced* an official-looking document on his word processor, walked into a London airport and (c) *passed through passport security / passed passport security through* without a single question. He even asked the security man the way, telling him that he was new to the job and didn't know how to get down to the staff room. Within 20 minutes he (d) *boarded / had boarded* a plane and was in the cockpit. At this point, as he didn't know how to fly the Jumbo 747, and (e) *not knowing / not known* how to operate the radio, he phoned the airport security office using his mobile phone and told them of his whereabouts. A spokesman for airport security said 'We wish (f) *to state / stating* here and now that security at London airport is second to none. We regret (g) *not to have stopped / not having stopped* the intruder but he used exceptional methods to enter the airport. Rarely (h) *does anyone get past / anyone gets past* our security checks and we would like to add that at no time (i) *there was / was there* any danger to the public.' The fancy dress uniform has (j) *been since returned / since been returned* to the shop.

4 There is a word missing from each of the sentences below. Add the missing word in the appropriate position.

a) Not only ^do they expect us to work all hours during the week, now they want us to come in on Saturday mornings!

b) When we were kids, we ^would climb into our neighbours' garden and steal apples.

c) As the problem needed an urgent solution, we spent all night looking into ^it very thoroughly.

d) In the end we gave up ^having tried everything we possibly could to improve the situation.

e) We went to that new Mongolian restaurant ^that opened last week.

f) I was sure I ^could smell smoke, but I really wasn't too sure where it was coming from.

g) If he ^had been paying a little more attention, he wouldn't have driven into the tree!

h) Gone are ^the days when we could leave our front door unlocked without worrying about intruders.

i) It has ^been widely recognised that stress in the workplace is increasing to dangerous levels.

j) He's a really nice guy, he ^will always have time to talk to you, no matter how busy he is.

k) I'd have said something, had ^I known that he'd insulted you like that!

l) We wish ^to inform you that the swimming pool will be closing at 9.30 pm as of 16 July.

5 Complete the conversation between two friends using an appropriate form of the verb in brackets. Use *will* or *would* where possible.

Gill: How are things going between you and Pete, these days? Last time I saw you, you told me about how he (a) _would always forget_ (always / forget) to tell you where he was or what time he was coming home, and how the two of you (b) _would have_ (have) arguments every weekend ...

Kate: Oh, that was ages ago! Yeah, things are fine now. He's being really nice actually. I (c) _will come_ (come) home sometimes and he (d) _'ll have prepared_ (prepare) the dinner with candles and wine and everything ...

Gill: Hey, that's great. So, what brought about the big change then?

Kate: Well, we (e) _sat_ (sit) down one evening and talked things through and we both admitted that we (f) _were_ (be) a bit stressed out at work and that we (g) _hadn't realised_ (realise) the effect it (h) _was having_ (have) on our relationship.

Gill: And since then there've been no more problems?

Kate: No, though I don't know what (i) _would have happened_ (happen) if we (j) _hadn't talked_ (not / talk) things out. I mean, it's not totally inconceivable that we (k) _would have split_ (split) up.

Gill: Wow! I had no idea it was so serious!

Kate: Yeah, it sobered us both up. I really don't know what I (l) _would have done_ (do) if he (m) _had left_ (leave) me.

Vocabulary

1 Complete the expressions with an appropriate preposition.

a) deep _in_ conversation

b) developed a taste _for_ something

c) _In_ very poor taste

d) _Under_ no circumstances

e) got a word _in_ edgeways

f) bear _in_ mind

g) _In_ two minds

2 Complete the sentences below using the expressions in 1.

a) She really doesn't know what to do. She's _in two minds_ about taking a year off or going straight to university.

b) I never _got a word in edgeways_. They were talking all the time and I never got a chance to say anything.

c) She tried Indian food the other day and now she's _developed a taste for_ it and keeps going to her local Indian restaurant.

d) When you _bear in mind_ that she's only 24, coming second in the round-the-world yacht race is a great achievement.

e) _Under no circumstances_ should you climb that mountain without the correct equipment and plenty of food and water.

f) When I walked into the room they were both _deep in conversation_. So I decided not to interrupt and let them continue talking.

g) I thought his joke was _in very poor taste_. It was completely inappropriate and everyone looked shocked.

3 Rewrite the following sentences using a phrase from the box. Make any changes that are necessary.

> take great pride in   bottle things up ~to add together several amounts / numbers in order to calculate the total.~
> sort it out   have enough   tot up the bill
> spring up   come up   identify with someone
> put things off   get close to

a) I never get down to work straightaway, I always procrastinate and waste time. _(v.) to delay doing sth. that you should do_

I never get down to work straightaway, I always put things off and waste time.

b) Look, things can't go on like this, you're really going to have to find a solution.

Look, things can't go on like this, you're really going to have to sort it out.

c) My mum feels very proud of her garden, she spends hours looking after it and it's a joy to see.

My mum takes great pride in her garden, she spends hours looking after it and it's a joy to see.

d) I can't help Tom because he keeps his problems to himself and just won't talk about them.

I can't help Tom because he bottles things up and just won't talk about them.

e) I thought the film was great. I really felt that the main character was very like me.

I thought the film was great. I really identified with the main character.

f) I'm thinking of resigning. I'm really fed-up.

I'm thinking of resigning. I've really had enough.

g) Listen, you're good at Maths, you work out how much we have to pay.

Listen, you're good at Maths, you tot up the bill.

h) Have you seen that new supermarket? It just seems to have appeared overnight.

Have you seen that new supermarket? It just seems to have sprung up overnight.

i) Your name was mentioned in a conversation I had with your boss last night.

Your name came up in a conversation I had with your boss last night.

j) I almost won the lottery last week. One more correct number and I'd have hit the jackpot!

I got close to winning the lottery last week. One more correct number and I'd have hit the jackpot!

4 Match the words in box A with the correct category in box B.

A

a) power   efficiency   achievement   competence

b) grubby   bustling   clogged   awe-inspiring

c) lengthy   pointless   predictable   animated

d) clench   peer   flit about   slip off

e) gut   flog   mucky   nick

f) mouth-watering   savoury   home-made   caramelised

B

1 c words to describe conversations
2 f adjectives to describe food
3 a values traditionally thought of as male
4 e informal language
5 b words to describe a city
6 d descriptive verbs

5 Complete the sentences with words from 4. Use one word from each of the six groups.

a) What an amazing city: massive buildings, bright lights, and the view over the harbour is incredible. It really is an _awe-inspiring_ city.

b) A lot of men crave ___power___ . They like to dominate situations and influence people's thoughts and actions.

c) The meeting didn't resolve any of the issues. It was a waste of time, totally ___pointless___ .

d) He took the medal and I saw him ___clench___ it tightly in his hand.

e) And for dessert we had these delicious _caramelised_ fruit sticks, you know, dipped in hot, melted sugar.

f) You know what kids are like, they just love getting ___mucky___ , playing around in mud, or smearing paint everywhere.

6 Complete the following sentences with an appropriate form of the words in brackets.

a) The barman refused to serve him until he produced some _identification_ (identity)

b) The dining room was very _tastefully_ (adv.) decorated in blue. (taste)

c) Sue's really nice isn't she? Friendly, ___talkative___ and she's always laughing. (talk)

d) I was very impressed by his speed and ___efficiency___ when he came round to fix my computer. (efficient)

e) That's just so typical of him not to have taken the price into _consideration_ when choosing the venue. After all, he never pays! (consider)

f) The play was so long and so slow, I swear I almost died of ___boredom___ (n.) ! (bore)

g) 'Let's just wait and see what happens next,' she said with a ___meaningful___ (a.) glance and a short laugh. (mean)

h) I hadn't seen Monica for twenty years. She'd dyed her hair blond and was totally _unrecognisable_ (a.) (recognise)

Pronunciation

1 ▭▭ Listen to these sentences. Is the speaker's tone:

a) enthusiastic (E)?
b) angry (A)?
c) neutral (N)?

1 You know that restaurant you told us about? We went there last night. ☐

2 I've just finished that text you gave me to correct. ☐

3 So, what are you doing tonight? Going out I suppose. ☐

4 It's been ages since I last went to the cinema. Let's go tonight. ☐

5 It's probably one of the best films ever made. ☐

6 So, your mother's coming round for dinner tonight? ☐

2 ▭▭ Read these three short jokes. Listen to the jokes and mark the main stresses.

a) A: Waiter, waiter, there's a fly in my soup!
   B: I'm really sorry sir, but we'll have to charge you extra for it!

b) A: Waiter, waiter, there's a fly in my soup!
   B: Could you just keep quiet about it sir, or everyone will want one!

c) A: Waiter, waiter, there's a fly in my soup!
   B: Really, what's he doing there?
   A: Breaststroke, I think.

▭▭ Listen again to check your answers. Then repeat the jokes along with the tape.

S + (adv.) + (a.) + N.
clause = (a.) + V.

8 Cyberspace

Cyber quiz

Are you a technophile or a technophobe? Do this quiz and find out. Then check your answers on page 88.

1. When was the first computer invented?
   a) 1936   b) 1951   c) 1974

2. Which company was the first to develop personal home-use computers?
   a) IBM   b) Macintosh   c) Microsoft

3. What does WWW mean?
   a) Working With the Web   b) Well Worked Web
   c) World Wide Web

4. Which country does the following site come from? http://www.outandabout.co.nz
   a) Norway   b) New Zealand
   c) The Netherlands

5. What does the 'e' in e-mail stand for?
   a) electrical   b) electronic   c) efficient

Grammar

1. Correct the mistakes in each of these sentences.
   a) I'll finish this exercise by the time the bell rings.
   b) This time tomorrow I'll sit on an airplane.
   c) In twenty years' time, most people will have used their TV as the screen for their computers.
   d) By the time I finish my computer course, I'll be spending over 10,000 pounds on tuition fees.
   e) Many scientists believe it's impossible that one day we live on other planets.
   f) I don't believe that computers will ever developed to be more intelligent than humans.
   g) Don't worry about moving to a new country, after six months you have made loads of friends.
   h) It's Saturday tomorrow, so I won't be probably going in to the office.

2. Complete these sentences with *will* and an appropriate infinitive form of the verb in brackets.
   a) By this time next week he 'll have finished (finish) the course.
   b) I suppose he 'll be (be) late as usual.
   c) I don't think he 'll have (have) enough money to buy that car.
   d) This time next week I 'll be starting (start) my new job.
   e) My car 'll be repaired (repair) by now so I'll just pop to the garage to pick it up.
   f) In the year 2010 more than 50% of the population will be working (work) in jobs connected with the Internet.
   g) If they continue selling like this, we will have sold (sold) a million copies of the CD by the end of the week.

3. Write predictions or assumptions based on the facts given below using *will* and the prompts in brackets.

   Example
   You know Sue has got a hard day at work today.
   (she / very tired / get home)
   She'll be very tired when she gets home.

   a) Richard usually plays football on Monday nights at 8 o'clock. It's Monday today. (he / at home / 8.30 he / football)
   He won't be at home at 8.30. He'll be playing football.
   b) The exercise only takes 10 minutes. It's 8.45 now. (you / finish the exercise / nine o'clock)
   You'll have finished the exercise by nine o'clock.
   c) The film you're watching is a typical action movie. (the good guys / win / and the bad guys / lose)
   The good guys 'll win and the bad guys 'll lose.
   d) Your brother is on holiday in the Caribbean. He loves diving. (he / probably dive / right now)
   He will probably be diving right now.
   e) It rains a lot in London. You're going there on holiday next week. (I / probably need / umbrella)
   I suggest you'll probably need an umbrella.

f) You took the film to the Photo shop yesterday. They offer a 24-hour photo development service. (my photos / probably develop / now)

My photos will probably be developed by now.

g) Maria is studying medicine. She's doing very well in her studies. She's only 23. (she / work as a doctor / time / thirty)

She'll be working as a doctor by the time she's thirty.

4 Use the discourse markers in the box to link the beginning of the statements in A to their endings in B. Use each discourse marker once only.

> but now   this has meant that   in this sense
> but probably more importantly   after all
> as well as

A

a)	Computers have helped put people in touch with each other _as well as (4)_
b)	The progress of the Internet is continually being exaggerated. *But now. After all*
c)	Clearly the Internet has increased the speed of communication. *But probably more importantly*
d)	All companies expect their workers to be computer literate. *This has meant that*
e)	Not only has the computer revolution meant that people can work from home, *after all but now*
f)	Less than 10% of the world's population has access to e-mail. *In this sense*

B

1	Cyberspace can be said to be the domain of a privileged elite.
2	with the introduction of the laptop they can work anywhere.
3	30% of the world's population don't have access to electricity, let alone access to a computer.
4	helping them work together, despite living in different cities or even countries.
5	it has drastically reduced its costs.
6	employees without computer skills are now finding it harder to get a job.

5 Complete the text with the discourse markers in the box.

> but for a calendar year   also   this means that
> but in contrast to   in this sense
> but, more importantly

*C*astaway, a new reality TV phenomenon, has recently hit our screens in many countries. The original programme was conceived in the UK. It was inspired by the incredible success of the *Big Brother* programmes around the globe, and sees a group of 36 people, representing a cross section of society, volunteering to inhabit a deserted village on a remote island. As in *Big Brother*, their every move will be filmed, recorded and broadcast, (a) *but in contrast to* *Big Brother*, the participants are not totally among strangers. They are allowed to participate as family groups and (b) *in this sense Castaway* is very different, showing a much broader slice of life, with children and older people getting to grips with the difficulties created by the isolation of living on a small island. Another major difference is that the castaways are to remain on the island not for ten weeks, (c) *but for a calendar year*, and there is no opting out possible. (d) *This means that* the families have to get on together for a whole year, (e) *but more importantly* for the TV company, it (f) *also* means that the viewers will now be glued to the box for a full twelve months and not just ten weeks.

Vocabulary

1 Circle the correct preposition in these expressions.

a) no limit *of* / **to** / *for*

b) a good chance *by* / *from* / **of**

c) have in store *from* / *of* / **for**

d) **at** / *in* / *on* the expense *to* / **of** / *from*

e) come up *by* / *in* / **against**

f) *in* / **for** / *at* economic reasons

g) the turn **of** / *at* / *on* the century

h) *at* /(by)/ *on* far the most

i) keep ahead *to* / *from* /(of)

2 Complete the following text with the correct expressions in 1.

At (1) _the turn of the century_ when people began to look back at the past hundred years, few mentioned the video game as being a major player in the 20th century. In fact there has been a huge increase in the sale of home consoles and now about half the population of western Europe has facilities to play games on their TV or computer.

The boom started with *Space Invaders* which was (2) _by far the most_ influential game on the market in the 1970's. This now seems very dated compared with the new 3D games and virtual reality systems on offer. There seems to be (3) _no limit to_ the complexity of the modern video game as the manufacturers battle it out to (4) _keep ahead of_ each other.

The problem is that children spend time on them (5) _at the expenses of_ other forms of recreation like sport. In Britain, the government has (6) _come up against_ a barrage of complaints from worried parents for not taking more decisive action. Video games are often extremely violent and one wonders what the manufacturers (7) _have in store for_ us next. The government has done very little (8) _for economic reasons_. The video games industry creates thousands of jobs and valuable revenue for the government. Recently, however, the government has changed its stance, and there's (9) _a good chance of_ legislation being put in place in the future.

3 Complete these sentences with words from the box.

> hyperlink   log on   graphics   home page
> server   attachment   inbox   search engine

a) When I turned on my computer I had five new e-mails in my _inbox_ .

b) _Graphics_ can take up a lot of space. Some pictures can be as big as 10 Megabytes.

c) If you want to go to the page about the cinema just click on the _hyperlink_ and you'll go straight to the page.

d) I didn't know any websites with information about inventors so I went to a _search engine_ and typed in the word 'Inventors'.

e) When you _log on_ to your computer you need to type in your password.

f) When you create a website you must send all your pages to a _server_ and that way other people can access your site.

g) He has changed his _home page_ . When you go to his site the first thing you see is a picture of his latest book and a menu list.

h) He added the picture to the e-mail and sent it as an _attachment_ .

4 Complete this crossword with words associated with computers, the Internet and e-mail.

```
                              N
      2 O N L I N E           E
                              T
                              W
  3 S O F T 4 W A R E   5 C   O
    U         E         H     R
    R       6 B O O K M A R K
    F         S         T
    I         I         R
    N         T         O
    G       7 N E W S G R O U P
                        M
```

Across

2   working on the Internet

3   computer programmes

6   to make a note of a site address on your computer

7   a site where people share information about a specific topic

Down

1   a group of computers linked to each other

3   visiting various different sites on the Web

4   where companies, individuals or organisations display information about themselves on the Net

5   a site where you can write to people by e-mail in real time

Listening & reading

1 Which of these things were invented in the 20th century?

Car
Internet
Television
Telephone
Train

2 🖭 You are going to listen to a radio debate concerning the greatest inventions of the past 200 years. Cover the tapescript and listen to the recording. Then check your answers to 1.

Interviewer: Good evening. Tonight we're debating whether the Internet was the greatest invention of the past two hundred years. On my left I have Sir Richard Hughes, who is head of Information Technology at London University, and alongside him Melissa Atwell, an IT expert and writer of several books on computer programming languages. On my right is Mark Daniels, a research scientist at Harvard and Pablo Perez, a well-known journalist and TV presenter.

Richard, I'd like to start with you. With so many great inventions to choose from, what makes you think the Internet was the most significant?

Richard: I think it is its impact on information. There's no doubt the telephone in the 19th century, and the television, in the 20th century, both had a massive effect on communication but the Internet empowered us all. The Internet means information for the masses. The television and the telephone are very much controlled by government and big business but the Internet was a kind of people's revolution. It meant that a large proportion of the population now has access to an infinite amount of information at the touch of a button. Not only that, but this information is worldwide.

Interviewer: Mark Daniels, would you like to counter that?

Mark: Ah, yeah, the Internet is significant but it wasn't until the 1990s that we really saw its effects. There have been other inventions that have had a greater effect on the way we live. The car, for example, invented in the 19th century, completely changed our way of living. We were able to move out of cities and we could travel with complete independence and look how it affected the environment we live in. Anyway, don't forget that the Net is dominated by English. If you don't speak English, its possibilities are a lot more limited.

Interviewer: Melissa Atwell have you anything to add?

Melissa: The car revolutionised transport or at least private transport. But don't forget we already had the train, people could get around before the car was invented. What is remarkable about the impact of the Internet was that it affected so many things. It changed education, the way we run business, our access to information, global communications ... For example, I regularly have meetings with my bosses in the USA and we hold our meeting across the Net. This has made the need for travel redundant. That is what is so powerful. It has redefined so much of what we do, it has made many of the great inventions of the 19th and 20th century less significant ...

Pablo: ... I disagree with all the comments so far ...

Interviewer: Sorry, Pablo, did you want to say something?

Pablo: Yes, for me television has made the greatest impact. Since the early 1970s, you can go to the poorest of countries in the middle of Africa and you'll find TVs, but you won't find the Internet. The TV is everywhere and it has affected the whole way we view entertainment and our whole concept of society. It has helped shape our national identity more than anything else. It is a major source of political, social and economic information. It shapes fashion, our ideas and even our morals. Its effect on our concept of society is nothing less than phenomenal.

Richard: Yes, but it's not as simple as that ...

3 🖭 Listen again. Which person do the following sentences refer to? Write RH (Sir Richard Hughes), MA (Melissa Atwell); MD (Mark Daniels) or PP (Pablo Perez).

a) Argues that the Internet has reduced the importance of other inventions in the last 200 years? *MA*

b) Believes that the car has not only had a massive impact on transport but also on the environment? *MD*

c) Points out that the Internet is not owned and run by governments or private business? *RH*

d) Maintains that the television has redefined society and influenced not only our thoughts but our morals as well? *PP*

e) Makes the point that to use the Internet most effectively you should speak English? *MD*

f) Stresses that the key issue is the information revolution and access to that information on a worldwide scale? *RH*

g) Highlights the multi-faceted nature of the Internet revolution and that its impact is in all areas of life, such as business, communication and education? *MA*

4 Complete the phrases in *italics* with the correct preposition. Check your answers with the tapescript on page 44.

a) I think it is its *impact __on__ information.*

b) ... infinite amount of information __at__ the *(touch) of a button.*

c) ... both *had a massive effect __on__* communication.

d) *What is remarkable __about__ the impact of the* Internet was ...

e) It is *a major source __of__ political, social* and economic information.

5 Complete the text with the phrases in *italics* and their dependent propositions in 4.

Another great invention, which really took off in the 20th century, was the camera. (a) __At the touch of a button,__ you can get an instant visual record. (b) __What is remarkable about__ the camera is that it has hardly changed in nearly 200 years. The same basic technique is still valid today. Though the camera hasn't (c) __had a massive effect__ the way we live, it has changed the way we record the past. Cameras and the photos they produce are (d) __a major source__ pleasure for millions of people around the world. What's more with the introduction of digital cameras their (e) __impact on__ future generations is virtually guaranteed.

Writing

1 Some people argue that the Internet was the greatest invention of the 20th century. Look at the Listening & reading section and read the summaries of the points the experts made in 3.

What do you consider to be the greatest invention of the 20th century? Choose an invention and write three reasons why you think it is the greatest invention of the 20th century.

Invention _____
Reasons why
1 _____
2 _____
3 _____

2 Which of the following things might the introduction to a discursive essay include?

a) An introduction to the topic, demonstrating why the topic area is worth considering ☐

b) Some of your arguments ☐

c) Your general opinion ☐

d) A basic repetition of the question ☐

e) Evidence to support your arguments ☐

f) A preview of your conclusion ☐

g) A list of detailed examples ☐

h) An outline of what you plan to say ☐

3 Read these two introductions and decide which one is the best. Use your checklist in 2 to help you.

a) Many people, looking back over the last part of the 20th century claim that the Internet has had a bigger impact on our lives than any other recent invention. I believe this to be a rather short-sighted view of our history. The car, the telephone and the television have all played a significant role in shaping our society. But when it comes to helping us record out past, I strongly believe there is only one candidate, the camera.

b) *Nowadays, the Internet plays a major role in many areas of our society. However I don't think it is as important as the camera. When we started using the camera we completely changed our way of recording the past. Nearly all families have got cameras and they are used to record weddings, anniversaries and special moments in people's lives. Before the camera people had to record the past with paintings and so that is why there are far fewer records of the period before the camera was invented.*

4 Complete the text with discourse markers from the box.

for the first time	but then	prior to
not only	in this sense	it also meant that
but with	as well as	

(a) __Not only__ did the camera change the way we record history (b) __it also meant that__ people from all walks of life could participate in creating historical documents for future generations. (c) __Prior to__ the invention of the camera nearly all visual recollections of the past were in the form of painting and drawings which tended to be commissioned by the nobility or for religion. There were far fewer documents of how normal life was lived. (d) __But with__ the introduction of the camera this all changed. (e) __For the first time__ people from all areas of life were able to document their lives.

5 Write an essay which answers this question using discourse markers from 4.

'What do you consider to be the most important invention of the 20th century?'

You should write approximately 250 words.

9 Law

Laws worldwide

Circle the correct words.

a) In London it's *allowed* / *illegal* / *legal* to drive a car while not sitting in the front seat.

b) Duelling is *prohibited* / *illegal* / *legal* in Paraguay as long as both parties are blood donors.

c) Every citizen in Kentucky is *required* / *prohibited* / *legal* to take a bath once a year.

d) In Massachusetts, snoring is *prohibited* / *required* / *allowed* unless all the bedroom windows are closed and securely locked.

e) In Switzerland, you are not *required* / *illegal* / *allowed* to hang out washing on Sundays.

Grammar

1 Read the following sentences and rephrase them using the modal verb in brackets.

Example
He's over an hour late, the only possible explanation is that he's forgotten about the appointment.

He must have forgotten about the appointment.

a) 'I really can't afford to buy a new car, it's far too expensive,' he explained.

~~He explained that he couldn't afford to buy a new car, it's far too expensive~~ (could)

b) She doesn't believe it was an accident, she has evidence to suggest that it was intentional.

~~She believes it might have been intentional~~ (might)

c) I told you to get the boiler checked. Now it doesn't work, it's freezing and it's the middle of winter.

~~You should have got the boiler checked. Now,~~ (should)

d) 'I'll make sure all the doors are locked and all the lights switched off,' Cathy promised.

~~Cathy promised that she would make sure all the doors are locked~~ (would) ~~and all the lights switched off~~

e) They can't be the ones who stole the money. They didn't have enough time.

~~They couldn't have stolen the money. They didn't have enough time~~ (could)

f) I'm sure he didn't know about your news, or he'd have said something.

~~He can't have known about your news or he'd have said sth~~ (can)

g) I'm disappointed that you didn't let us know you were coming to town last weekend.

~~You could have let us know you're coming to town last weekend~~ (could)

2 Complete the dialogue with the correct modal.

Glen: Hi, Alan, you know that money I lent Giles, well, he promised he (a) ~~would~~ pay back the loan within three weeks, but he (b) ~~must~~ have forgotten.

Alan: Well, didn't I warn you not trust him? You (c) _____ have made him write you out a cheque, then you (d) ~~could~~ have avoided all these problems.

Glen: Well, you never know, he (e) ~~may~~ have genuinely forgotten.

Alan: Well, I think it's more likely that it's slipped his mind because it suits him. Anyway, didn't he say he (f) ~~would~~ come over to see us this weekend? Well, where is he?

Glen: Yes, you're right. I (g) ~~should~~ have insisted that he gave me a cheque.

3 Each of the following sentences has one word missing. Insert the missing word.

a) I'm really sorry, I have been looking where I was going.

b) She promised she phone if there were any problems.

c) I know I really ought have phoned sooner, but I was really busy.

d) His phone was engaged, I suppose he might have been checking his e-mail.

e) I thought he'd have arrived by now, he must be got stuck in the traffic.

f) Why's the light still on? You should have been asleep by now!

g) You should have told me there was no food in the house, I ~~have~~ gone to the shops.
   ^might, should, could

h) I'm sorry, I really don't know where it is. I suppose I might have left it at home.

HW

4 Match the beginnings of the sentences in box A with the endings in box B.

A

a)	He was so disappointed with the outcome of the court case
b)	She wasn't expecting to get the job
c)	He hates the fact that he has to work on the night shift
d)	There was such confusion over the new voting system
e)	He has such a bad reputation for not paying his debts
f)	She was neither happy to help

B

e	1	that no one will lend him any money.
c	2	and his wife, who has to spend the evenings alone, does too.
f	3	nor was she willing to say why.
b	4	and she certainly didn't expect to be offered such a generous salary.
a	5	that he decided to give up practising law.
d	6	that many people voted for the wrong candidate.

HW

5 Rewrite the sentences in 4 beginning with the word/s given below: was he

a) So disappointed with the outcome of the court case, he decided to give up practising law.

b) She wasn't expecting to get the job nor was she expect to be offered such a generous salary.

c) He hates the fact that he has to work on the night shift and so does his wife who has to spend the evenings alone.

d) Such was confusion over the new voting system that many people voted for the wrong candidate.

e) So bad reputation for not paying his debts that no one will lend him any money.

f) Neither was she happy to help nor was she willing to say why.

Vocabulary

HW

1 Choose the correct answer.

a) Which of these punishments would a judge probably not give in court?
   1 fine 2 suspended sentence
   ③ solitary confinement 4 imprisonment

b) Which one of these crimes involves fire?
   1 kidnapping 2 swearing in public
   ③ arson 4 fraud

c) Which one of these is the least serious crime?
   1 fraud 2 manslaughter 3 mugging
   ④ graffiti

d) What is the word used for the outcome of a court case?
   1 result 2 decision ③ verdict
   4 conclusion

e) Which one of these crimes involves driving?
   ① speeding 2 fraud 3 libel
   4 dropping litter

f) Which one of these crimes is not a form of theft?
   1 mugging 2 shop-lifting 3 burglary
   ④ trespassing

2 Complete these expressions to do with law with the words from the box.

above by down into unto with

a) a law unto himself
b) lay down the law
c) taking the law into your own hands
d) is above the law
e) by law
f) in trouble with the law

3 Choose the most appropriate expressions from 2 to complete the sentences below.

1 It's up to the police to control crime. There's no point in taking the law into your own hands.

2 The police are always going round to his parents' house. He's constantly in trouble with the law.

3 Her father really used to lay down the law. He would order her to be home by 11 pm.

4 He acts as if he is above the law and can get away with anything, but one day he'll find himself in big trouble.

5 When it comes to driving, Tony's a law unto himself. He's always driving over the speed limit and jumping the lights.

6 The playing of music on the underground is prohibited by law.

4 Match the formal words from column A with their more neutral forms from column B. Then use the words from column A to complete the following newspaper headlines.

A _(before sth.)_   B
a) Prior to   1 started
b) Prominent _(a) well known_ 5   2 very bad
c) Seeking 7   3 in addition
d) Severe 2 _(adv.) in addition to_   4 before
e) Further 3   5 well-known
f) Depict _to show_ 8   6 later
g) Commenced _(v.) to begin_ 1   7 asking for
h) In due course   8 show

1 _Severe_ flooding hits southern France. Hundreds homeless over night.

2 _Prominent_ politician loses driving licence in drink driving scandal.

3 Shock photos _depict_ prince as tropical playboy.

4 _Number of refugees_ _seeking_ _asylum in Europe grows._

5 **Mayor caught in bribe scandal** _prior to_ **election.**

Pronunciation

Read these sentences and decide if the underlined consonant is pronounced or not. Circle the consonants that are pronounced.

a) Wha_t_ di_d_ Tom say?
b) I_t_ is the firs_t_ turning on the righ_t_, isn'_t_ it?
c) He trippe_d_ over the wire an_d_ fell.
d) I shouldn'_t_ have sai_d_ anything.
e) They lef_t_ it down a_t_ the police station.
f) He didn'_t_ mean to do i_t_.
g) I couldn'_t_ believe tha_t_ she was innocen_t_.
h) Tha_t_ was the las_t_ thing he sai_d_ to me.
i) He turne_d_ on the ligh_t_ an_d_ checke_d_ the time.

Listen to check your answers. Practise reading the sentences aloud.

Listening & reading

1 Listen to two friends discussing the problems involved in doing jury service. (If you don't have the recording, read the tapescript on page 79.) Make a note of what they think is:

a) the main problem

_____

_____

b) the main reason for doing jury service

_____

_____

2 Complete these extracts from the conversation with an appropriate preposition.

a) ... more and more people are trying to _get_ _____ of it if they can.

b) ... there's a problem about _taking time_ _____ _work._

c) ... they don't actually have to pay your wages when you're _____ _jury service_ ...

d) ... it's much less than most people earn _____ _work_ ...

e) I mean it sounds like a good thing to do _____ _theory_ ...

f) ... but if you're going _to be_ _____ _of pocket_ ... well ...

g) ... that seems to be what's _____ _the root of_ the problem.

Listen again (or read the tapescript on page 79) to check your answers.

3 Complete the sentences below with expressions from 2. Make any changes that are necessary.

a) It's been such a long time since I last _____ that I've forgotten what a holiday is!

b) They are always arguing about silly little things, but it's obvious there must be something more serious _____ their arguments.

c) Never having to do another day's work sounds great _____ , but wouldn't it be a bit boring in the long run?

d) He's really naughty, he's always looking for excuses to _____ doing his homework.

e) Being _____ is an enriching experience and you feel that you are fulfilling your role as a responsible citizen.

f) Considering we spend approximately 60% of our waking hours _____ , it's important to have a job that you enjoy.

g) He threw a superb party and invited all his friends, but it left him a bit _____ for the rest of the month.

4 Look at the headline of the newspaper report on page 49 about jurors' attitudes to doing jury service. Do you think their attitudes will be generally positive or negative? Read the article and find out.

Jury duty acquitted of first-degree hassle

By THEO EMERY, Associated Press

1 A Boston newspaper for attorneys surveyed jurors and found that once they were involved in the case they generally enjoyed weighing up the evidence and took the judgement of their peers seriously. More than 80 percent of respondents to the poll, published in Monday's edition of *Lawyers Weekly*, said the experience was positive, and some said it renewed their faith in the legal system.

2 Publisher David L. Yas was surprised by the results of the survey, which he said was the first of its kind. 'Most people dread jury duty,' Yas said. 'What we found is that once people get in there, they're intrigued by the case, energised by jury duty, and overall find jury duty quite positive.'

3 In Massachusetts, it is illegal for attorneys to speak with jurors even after a court case, so the survey was administered by judges. With the permission of State Jury Commissioner Frank Davis and Superior Court Chief Justice Suzanne V. Del Vecchio, 30 judges gave out surveys to jurors in superior court cases. About 130 people responded. All responses were voluntary and anonymous. The cases ranged from contract disputes to medical malpractice to first degree murder. One involved a lawsuit about a dog biting another dog.

4 The survey asked an array of questions about courtroom tactics, the condition of the courthouse, the appearance and demeanour of lawyers and court employees, the use of witnesses and exhibits, and the jurors' overall impression of the system.

5 Respondents reported not sleeping at night because of the gravity of the case, feeling proud of being part of the justice system, and finding the whole process to be a learning experience. 'Our justice system may not be perfect, but it works and I am proud to have served,' one respondent wrote. Another wrote: 'After several cases such as the O.J. Simpson trial, I lost all respect for the system. This case helped restore my respect for the system. There is hope for us.'

6 About 20 percent of the returned surveys were negative. 'It was not only a waste of my time, but the compensation was ridiculous,' one juror wrote. Another complained about having to clean up the jury room and pay for parking and gas and said jurors should be treated with more respect.

7 Yas said he has not been on a real jury, only a jury at a mock trial for middle school students. But even that case, which involved vehicular homicide charges against a woman who ran over a man after a concert, was riveting, he said. 'It was tremendous,' he said. 'We probably could have gone on for hours.'

BOSTON (August 14, 2000)

---

5 Are the following statements true or false?

a) A large majority of the people questioned found the experience generally very positive. [T]

b) Some jurors complained about the behaviour of the lawyers. [F]

c) More than a quarter of those surveyed responded negatively. [F]

d) Generally people's attitudes to jury duty change once they've experienced it. [T]

e) The publisher of the report had himself once been a juror. [F]

f) One respondent complained that they were not paid well enough. [T]

g) Some of the jurors found the responsibility quite stressful. [T]

h) All of the respondents reported feeling proud of their role in the justice system. [F]

6 Find words in the article which mean:

a) people who are doing something with you, or who are of a similar age or social status (paragraph 1) _peers_

b) the survey (paragraph 1) _poll_

c) not to look forward to doing something (paragraph 2) _dread_

d) to be given energy and enthusiasm (paragraph 2) _energised_

e) lawyers (paragraph 3) _attorneys_

f) answered (paragraph 3) _responded_

g) behaviour (paragraph 4) _demeanor_

h) seriousness (paragraph 5) _gravity_

i) a simulation of a real situation (paragraph 7) _mock_

j) fascinating (paragraph 7) _tremendous_

7 Complete the following newspaper report with some of your answers from 6.

In a recent (a) _poll_ , office workers were asked to list the things that most annoyed them about their jobs. A majority of the respondents reported (b) _dread_ going to work on a Monday morning, and more than 50% said that their jobs no longer (c) _energised_ them. One of their greatest fears was that of being passed over for promotion in favour of one of their (d) _peers_ , whilst the main worry for female employees was the attitude of some of the older male executives to their role in the office. As many as 65% of the women (e) _responded_ positively to the question, 'Do you feel discriminated against at work?', although only 1.5% of these women had sought the help of (f) _attorneys_ and taken their case to court.

Writing

You are going to write the text for a radio news report on crime. Here are some of the figures you have researched.

Re-offending statistics   *commit crime again*

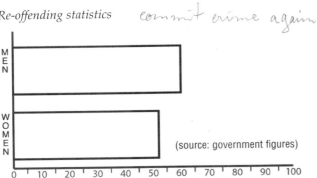

(source: government figures)

Types of crimes committed by re-offenders

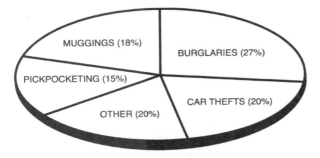

MUGGINGS (18%)
BURGLARIES (27%)
PICKPOCKETING (15%)
OTHER (20%)
CAR THEFTS (20%)

REASONS FOR RE-OFFENDING: No possibility of getting a job, boredom, lack of money.

TRAINING: of prisoners who receive job training (e.g. IT or construction), 60% find work when released.

EMPLOYMENT: Only 20% of ex-prisoners who find stable employment re-offend.

---

1   Look at the figures and complete these sentences.

a)   _58_ % of men who go to prison for 12 months re-offend within 12 months.

b)   _48_ % of women who go to prison for 12 months re-offend within 12 months.

c)   The commonest crime for re-offenders is _burglaries_

d)   _Muggings_ account for 18% of crimes by re-offenders.

e)   Prisoners often re-offend because they cannot get a _job_ .

f)   Amongst prisoners who go on job training programmes, _40_ % do not find work when they are released.

g)   Amongst prisoners who find _stable employment_, 80% do not re-offend.

2   Look at the following useful expressions. Decide if you would use each one to

a)   refer to information.
b)   make comparisons.
c)   draw conclusions.

	a	b	c
according to …	✓		
compared with …		✓	
in contrast, …		✓	
in general, …			✓
government statistics show that …	✓		
overall, …			✓
on the whole, …			✓
whereas …		✓	
in conclusion, …			✓

3   Write your report. It should be no longer than 250 words. Start with a brief introduction and then cover the following points in whatever order seems best to you.

a)   the percentage of re-offenders amongst men and women

b)   reasons why people re-offend

c)   a suggestion of what the government could do to help reduce the figures

d)   the types of crimes they commit when they re-offend

10 Firsts

Famous firsts

> the Lumière brothers   Alexander Graham Bell
> Marie Curie   Robert Edwin Peary
> Wilbur and Orville Wright
> Edmund Hillary and Tenzing Norgay

Complete these sentences with the names from the box.

a) *Alexander Graham Bell* produced the first telephone cable capable of transmitting and receiving human speech.

b) *Edmund Hillary + Tenzing Norgay* were the first climbers to reach the summit of Mount Everest.

c) *Wilbur + Orville Wright* were the first people to make a successful flight in a craft heavier than air.

d) *Marie Curie* first developed X-ray treatment.

e) *Robert Edwin Peary* is generally credited with being the first man to reach the North Pole.

f) *The Lumière brothers* were responsible for developing the first cinema.

Grammar

1 Complete the texts with *but*, *however* or *whereas*.

> Cross-country skiing is considered one of the best all-round sports workouts. It exercises all the main muscle groups and (a) _*whereas*_ jogging can cause stress injuries, cross-country skiing doesn't as the action involved is one of gliding. Swimming, of course, is also considered to be a good all-round workout, (b) _*but*_ it tends to overwork arm and shoulder muscles and can result in a 'triangular' physique. (c) _*However*_ , if what you are looking for is a slim, toned silhouette, then look no further. Cross-country skiing is the sport for you.

> My family is pretty competitive. We love playing all sorts of games, and coming first is *really* important. My favourite is probably Monopoly
> (d) _*whereas*_ my brother prefers Risk.
> (e) _*However*_ , mum's favourite game is Trivial Pursuit and I always want to be in her team as she always knows all the answers.

> It has been suggested that introducing tests for pre-school children could seriously affect their psychological development. (f) _*Whereas*_ older children are better able to cope with competition, the instinct to come first has not yet developed in children under four. Forcing them to face the possibility of failure can make them reserved and there have even been cases of children as young as four suffering from pre-test stress. (g) _*But*_ , despite this, the government is still going ahead with plans to introduce entry tests for primary schools.

2 Use the discourse markers in the box to link the beginning of the statements in box A to their endings in box B. Use each discourse marker twice.

Example
Swimming constantly for an hour without stopping is very good for building up your stamina but it can be incredibly boring.   *(bory) compare or contrast two facts*

> (whereas)   but   however

A

> a) Swimming constantly for an hour without stopping is very good for building up your stamina 3
> b) I've never liked taking part in competitions 6 *whereas*
> c) Some people prefer to go swimming in the sea 5 *whereas*
> d) The first time I saw the film I really didn't understand anything 1 *however*
> e) When you're learning something new for the first time, it's really exhausting 4 *however*
> f) You're supposed to think that it's taking part that's important 2 *but*

B

> 1 the second time it was much clearer.
> 2 to be perfectly honest I get much more of a buzz out of winning!
> 3 it can be incredibly boring.
> 4 once you've mastered it, you expend much less energy.
> 5 I prefer the fresh-water swimming in a river or a lake.
> 6 my brother really thrives on them.

3 Complete the sentences using the correct form of the words in brackets.

[handwritten: opportunity or a chance]

a) Make the most of your stay, it'll be a long time before you _get to visit_ such a beautiful spot again. (get / visit)

[handwritten: persuade]

b) They _got him to accept_ the job even though he really wasn't interested. (get / him / accept)

[handwritten: activity]

c) He _got computer working_ but only after changing the hard drive. (get / computer / work)

[handwritten: success]

d) I think she's working really well and could _get to be_ line manager in the next year or so. (get / be)

[handwritten: passive]

e) It was quite cheap to _get the car repaired_. I thought it was going to cost more. (get / car / repair)

[handwritten: activity]

f) They were a little quiet at first but the music soon _got them dancing_. (get / them / dance)

[handwritten: persuade]

g) We pointed out that the jacket had a mark on it and _we got them to reduce_ the price by 20%. (get / them / reduce)

[handwritten: passive]

h) Everybody was really surprised when the champion _got beaten_ by a complete unknown. (get / beat)

4 Rewrite these sentences with *get* or an expression with *get*. You may have to make changes to the sentence structure.

a) Let's start, shall we, or we'll be late.
[handwritten: Let's get going, shall we, or we'll be late.]

b) Although it was bit disappointing to start with, the film became better as it went on.
[handwritten: Although it was bit disappointing to start with, the film got better as it went on.]

c) Did you know that Luke's radio was stolen from his car the other day?
[handwritten: Did you know that Luke's radio got stolen from his car the other day?]

d) I finally succeeded in seeing Madonna in concert after queuing for tickets all night.
[handwritten: I finally got to see Madonna in concert after queuing for tickets all night.]

e) Anita graduated from Cardiff University and went on to work in the civil service.
[handwritten: Anita got a degree from Cardiff University and went on to work in the civil service.]

f) Barbara is very good at persuading other people to do all her dirty work.
[handwritten: Barbara is very good at getting other people to do all her dirty work.]

g) We went to see that new comedy at the Regent. It was really good, it made us both laugh.
[handwritten: We went to see that new comedy at the Regent. It was really good, it got us both laughing.]

h) I asked the mechanic to repair my old car before I sold it.
[handwritten: I got the mechanic to repair my old car before I sold it.]

5 Correct the mistakes in these sentences.

[handwritten: passive]

a) She gets her clothes clean *[handwritten: cleaned]* at the dry cleaner's.

[handwritten: activity]

b) Don't you worry, it's nothing serious, just do these exercises and we'll get you walk *[handwritten: to walking]* again very soon.

c) She got her bag stealing *[handwritten: stolen]* when she was in the cinema.

d) He got to arrest *[handwritten: arrested]* for shoplifting.

e) The group were very quiet to start with but once the discussion turned to politics we got them all talk. *[handwritten: all talking]*

[handwritten: succeed]

f) I'll never forget the time I got flying *[handwritten: to fly]* a plane on my own for the first time.

[handwritten: persuade]

g) I'm sure you can get her seen *[handwritten: to see]* your side of the story.

[handwritten: start]

h) Right, you have an hour and a half to finish the exam, so good luck and get to write! *[handwritten: writing]*

Pronunciation

1 Look at these verbs and underline the stressed syllable. Listen to the recording to check your answers.

inaugurate	invite
celebrate	record
compete	recognise
contest	initiate

2 Complete the following sentences with nouns formed from the verbs in 1. Underline the stressed syllable in these nouns.

a) Public _____ and fame are often more important than cash prizes.

b) She won the race in an incredible time, beating all previous _____ by ten seconds.

c) A grand gala evening was organised for the _____ of the new town hall.

d) A certain element of _____ makes any game more interesting and fun to play.

e) Toys such as dolls houses or model cars can often represent a child's earliest _____ into the rituals of the adult world.

f) Free _____ were sent out to all the friends and families of the competing athletes.

g) The traditional _____ at the end of a race involves opening a magnum of champagne and spraying it over the crowd.

h) Television programmes such as quiz shows and talent _____ have been blamed for lowering the standards of broadcasting.

📼 Listen to the recording to check your answers.

Vocabulary

1 Rewrite the sentences below using the expressions from the box. Make any changes that are necessary.

> once in a lifetime   mass production
> against the clock   high profile   ardent fan
> the precise details of   multi-million pound

a) I don't know exactly what happened in the accident.

I don't know the precise details of the accident.

b) He's a very well-known government minister and is always in the news.

He's a very high profile government minister and is always in the news.

c) He needs to run the distance in 20 seconds. It'll be a race that's timed.

He needs to run the distance in 20 seconds. It'll be a race against the clock.

d) Henry Ford was the first man to organise the construction of cars in large numbers.

Henry Ford was the first man to organise the mass production of cars.

e) He'll never get another chance like this one. It's a unique opportunity.

He'll never get another chance like this one. It's once in a lifetime opportunity.

f) He's such an enthusiastic supporter of Manchester United that he's even named his son after the goalkeeper.

He's such an ardent fan of M. U.

g) He's been offered a very lucrative contract that will make him the richest footballer in Europe.

He's been offered a multi-million pound that ...

2 Complete these sentences with a phrase which includes *first*.

a) It really was a _first class_ meal. However, the service left a lot to be desired.

b) The wife of the president of the United States is sometimes referred to as America's _first lady_.

c) He's a very experienced pilot who has _first-hand_ knowledge of the area due to his time spent here in the war.

d) French is actually not his mother tongue. His _first language_ is Spanish. Both of his parents were born in Seville.

e) Fortunately Jane knew something about _first aid_. She managed to resuscitate the boy while waiting for the ambulance to arrive.

f) She's always especially nervous on the _first night_ of a new play.

g) If we want to travel while it's still cool we'll have to leave at _first light_, then we could be there before it gets too hot.

3 Put this text in the correct order.

a) People who insist on trying to take on the world's great geographical [1]

b) their goal. However, they argue that it's worth it, as it's only in this way that mankind can hope to make [8]

c) their lives in danger and to push [6]

d) by a very strong need to prove [4]

e) progress. [9]

f) their bodies to their limits, often to the detriment of their health, and certainly to the detriment of their personal relationships, in order to achieve [7]

g) challenges, such as climbing Everest or sailing around the world single- [2]

h) themselves and their worth. They are ready to put [5]

i) handed, must surely be driven [3]

4 Complete the sentences below by using an appropriate form of a verb from box A and a word from box B. Where necessary put the objects in brackets in the appropriate place.

A

| ask   run   be   pick   pluck   spring |

B

| up   off   out   around   to   up |

a) When I was young I used to _____ all day long and never felt tired. Nowadays I take life a lot more slowly.

b) My parents are coming back from Greece tomorrow and they want me to _____ (them) at the airport.

c) I was really nervous about asking him for his autograph. Anyway, I finally_____ the courage and he was fine.

d) Jon worked as an airline pilot and _____ somewhere different every week.

e) He went straight up to her and _____ (her) and she said yes.

f) When I think of Shirley, what _____ mind is how calm she always is.

Reading

1 You are going to read about Donald Campbell, the first person to hold both the land-speed and water-speed records at the same time. As you read, answer the following questions.

a) What were his fastest speeds? _276 mph_

b) In which year did he first hold both records? _Dec, 1964_

c) What sacrifice did he have to make in an attempt to achieve his final record? _His life_

d) In what ways was Donald's life similar to his father's? _____

Donald Campbell was the first man to hold both the land-speed and water-speed records at the same time. He was the son of Malcolm Campbell, who had collected a number of land-speed and water-speed records. At the beginning of the twentieth century, land speeds had begun to rise dramatically and by 1904, land speeds had reached the 100 mph mark (160 kph) for the first time. Malcolm Campbell

achieved his first land-speed record on 25 September 1924 when he drove his Sunbeam Bluebird at the incredible speed of 146 mph (235 kph). He attained nine more world land-speed records, raising the record to over 300 mph (483 kph) in 1935. Two years later he set the water-speed record at 141 mph (227 kph) which he held until he died of a stroke in 1948.

Though initially reluctant to follow in his father's footsteps, Donald was encouraged to take an interest in his father's endeavours and was gradually convinced by Leo Villa, a member of the Malcolm Campbell team, to pick up where his father had left off. At first Donald was more interested in setting new water-speed records. He decided to upgrade his father's boat, the K4. The team worked on designing a more sophisticated craft, the K7, which was more stable than the original. They subsequently created seven new water-speed records between 1955 and 1964, reaching a maximum speed of 276 mph (444 kph), what was to be his personal best water-speed record, at Lake Dumbleyung in Australia.

During this time, Donald started to develop an interest in the land-speed record too. Throughout his career he used only two cars, the first, 'the Bluebird', was destroyed in a crash in Utah in 1960. Donald was lucky to come out of the crash alive. The second car, also called 'the Bluebird', was similar in design to the first car but had a tailfin added to it to stabilise it at high speeds. This, however, meant that the vehicle was much less manoeuvrable and could only steer four degrees to the left or right. In December 1964, the same year in which he broke the water-speed record, he set a new land-speed record of 403 mph (648 kph) in his new Bluebird and became the first and only person to hold both speed records.

Donald Campbell always claimed to have psychic powers and superstition played a major part in his life. In 1967, he predicted his own death stating that his new world record attempt, which was to take place the following day, was doomed. The next day, while attempting to be the first man to go more than 300 mph (482 kph) on water, his boat shot out of the lake, somersaulted and disintegrated on impact with the water. Later it was confirmed that he had indeed achieved yet another record, but this time he had paid the ultimate price.

to break into one piece

to turn over comple in the a

2 Are these sentences true (T) or false (F)?

a) Donald's father died trying to break a water-speed record. F

b) Land speeds began to get dramatically faster at the beginning of the last century. T

c) Donald was not interested in pursuing his father's career at first. T

d) Donald used the same speedboat that his father had used without any modification. F

e) Changes were made to his second 'Bluebird' so that it could turn more effectively. T

f) Donald predicted his own death. T

3 Complete the expressions below with an appropriate form of the verbs in the box.

> play pick take pay follow

a) to follow in his father's footsteps
b) to take an interest in his father's endeavours
c) to pick up where his father left off
d) played a major part in his life
e) paid the ultimate price

4 Which one of the following verbs can you *not* use with the noun *record*?

> attain hold set break do achieve create

Look back at the text and check your answers to 3 and 4.

Writing

1 Read this newspaper report about how a third member of the Campbell family is keeping the tradition alive in the 21st century. Then answer these questions:

a) What record was he trying to break?

_____

b) Did he succeed?

_____

c) What are his plans for the future?

_____

Time And Tide Wait For No Man But Bluebird Still Hits 128mph (206kph)

Steve Dube

1 HISTORY was revisited as a new British land-speed record was set at the weekend.

2 Don Wales, grandson of 1920s world land-speed record-breaker Sir Malcolm Campbell, drove his Bluebird Electric car at an average speed of 128 mph (206 kph) at Pendine Sands, near St Clears, on Saturday. But his aim of breaking one of his grandfather's earlier records of 146 mph (235 kph) on the same sands was frustrated by the tide and the condition of the beach.

3 It was a clear, summer's day at low tide and the Bluebird shimmered in the heat haze, a truly impressive figure. The team members stood anxiously watching as the great machine gained acceleration and seemed to fly across the sand. To an untrained eye, the speed seemed impossible and I was convinced that the car was going to sprout wings and take off at any moment.

4 Mr Wales said, 'We're all really delighted and we had a great party to celebrate. The car was still accelerating as we came out of the designated distance which means we were well on course to equal my grandfather's record. But we had 500 metres less of the beach than expected because part of the sand at the eastern end was extremely wet and very rough, with large potholes and what looked like a river going over the surface. During the trials the day before the sand was fine, but you get a different beach at Pendine every morning.'

5 The team plans to return to Pendine in August for a new attempt on the 146 mph (235 kph) record. Eventually it is hoped to equal the speed of 174 mph (280 kph), which was Sir Malcolm Campbell's top speed at Pendine in 1927.

2 Match the paragraphs in the newspaper report to the following summaries:

a) a description of the day and the record being broken   3
b) an explanation of the headline   1
c) the team's plans for the future   5
d) a quotation from the record-breaker   4
e) the background to the story   2

3 You are going to <u>write a short newspaper report</u> about an <u>attempt to break a similar record</u>, the world wind-powered speed record on ice. Follow the instructions below.

1   Read through all the following instructions once before you start writing. Make notes on the information you are going to include and any useful language you may need, but do not start writing your article until you have a clear picture of the story.

2   Choose from the following headlines:

> **Kings sets new record for wind-powered speed.**

strong plow wind plow

> **Racing against the wind: ice speed record attempt fails**

> **High speed skating – the Windjet breaks another record!**

3   Write a one sentence sub-heading explaining the headline and summarising the main facts of the story.

4   Use the following information to help you write a short description of the attempt and the team:

air go in the front of the engine

air movement liquid fluel →

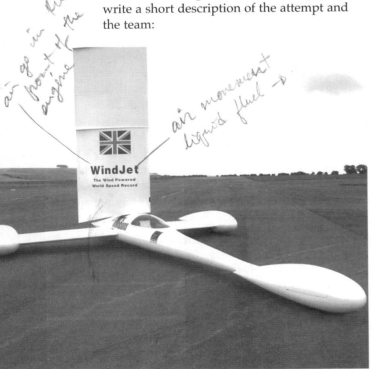

WindJet
The Wind Powered
World Speed Record

> **previous record:**
> 145 mph (233 kph)
>
> **target speed:**
> 180 mph (290 kph) – the fastest naturally powered human on earth
>
> **driver:**
> 28 year old Eddie Kings, former stunt man

5   Use the following information to help you write a description of the scene and the record-breaking attempt:

> **location:** Castle Rock Lake (Quincy Wisconsin). 17 miles (27 kilometres) long, 2 miles (3 kilometres) wide, very smooth surface as water is only ten feet deep
>
> **ideal conditions:** – 12 degrees, clear day, constant wind
>
> **procedure:** *hit, beat*
> the Windjet timed over a distance of a mile (1.6 kilometres)
> Speed reached: 167 mph (269 kph)

6   Report the <u>record-breaker's reactions</u> in direct speech. You may want to use some of the phrases from the box in 7 below.

7   Use this information to help you write a short paragraph about the team's plans for the future. You may want to use some of the phrases from the box.

> *personal reactions:*
> It's an incredible sensation …
> We're really proud of Eddie …
> We're delighted with today's result but …
> It's a team effort and I'd like to thank …
>
> *reporting future plans:*
> Not satisfied with establishing a new record …
> Having got so far, they are not about to give up …
> And the next step? To make an attempt on the …
> The team is now looking into the possibilities of …
> Target speed: 180 mph (290 kph)
> Date of new attempt: in three months' time

4 Use your notes to write up the newspaper report. You should write about 250 words.

11 Stories

A mini urban myth

Put the sentences in the correct order to form an urban myth.

a) Annoyed by this, and a little suspicious, the man checked his pocket and noticed that his wallet was missing. `2`

b) His wife replied, 'I know. You left your wallet on the table.' `8`

c) He quickly caught up with him and tackled him, yelling, 'Give me that wallet!'. `4`

d) A man went jogging in the park one morning when another jogger accidentally bumped into him, apologised and then jogged away. `1`

e) When the man returned home his wife asked him if he'd remembered to go to the supermarket. `6`

f) He immediately turned around and ran after the pickpocket. `3`

g) Anxious to tell her his story, he said, 'No, but I have a good excuse!' `7`

h) The frightened pickpocket gave it to him and ran off as quickly as he possibly could. `5`

Grammar

1 Match the story sections a–e with the extracts 1–5.

a) introduction `3`
b) background `5`
c) problem `4`
d) resolution `1`
e) comment `2`

d **1** The beautiful princess bent over and kissed him on the top of his head and he was instantly <u>transformed</u> into a handsome prince.

e **2** And so she sat down to dinner with her grandmother and the woodcutter and thought no more of the big bad wolf.

a **3** Once upon a time in a faraway land there lived a Prince who was looking for a wife.

c **4** As soon as the needle pricked her finger, she fell into a deep, deep sleep, from which she would only wake if kissed by a man who truly loved her.

b **5** The old carpenter was feeling very sad and lonely and as he bent over his work a single tear trickled down his cheek.

Now match the extracts to the fairy tales.

a) Sleeping Beauty `4`
b) Little Red Riding Hood `2`
c) Cinderella `3`
d) Pinocchio `5`
e) The Princess and the Frog `1`

2 Match the beginning of the sentences in box A to their endings in box B.

A

a)	It was supposed to have been the happiest day of their lives
b)	He was due to fly to Amsterdam for the opening of his new film
c)	The elections were due to take place in January
d)	She was to have gone into hospital for an operation
e)	They were on the verge of cancelling the whole show because of a strike
f)	They promised they would have the money ready

B

1	but, when he arrived at the bank to collect it, they had forgotten all about it.
2	but luckily the union came to an agreement with the management just in time.
3	but it was spoilt by the appearance of the bride's ex-husband, demanding that the ceremony be called off.
4	but the President changed his mind and rescheduled them for May.
5	but, at the last minute, she was told that it had to be postponed because there was no surgeon available.
6	but, in the end, he made the excuse that he was ill.

(handwritten left of box B: f, e, a, c, d, b)

3 Circle the correct form of the verb.

We were due (a) *meeting* / *to meet* at ten but something had obviously gone wrong. The clock hand now showed ten fifteen and I started to feel a little apprehensive, after all we were supposed (b) *catching* / *to be catching* the ten thirty train. We (c) *were going to run* / *'d run* away together to start a new life as far away from here as possible. I tried to remember exactly what we'd said. He'd

told me that he (d) *'d be waiting* / *was waiting* for me opposite the clock, but there was absolutely no sign of him. He'd imagined that I (e) *was* / *would be* the one to be late. I looked around to see if there was another clock, but there wasn't. The time ticked by. The train was due (f) *to leave* / *leaving*. What could have happened? Had he changed his mind? (g) *Was he going to* / *Was he due to* abandon me? It was nearly ten twenty-nine now, the bustle of the station was beginning to get on my nerves. I was on the verge of (h) *giving up* / *to give up* when I saw him, running across the forecourt towards me, his arms outstretched, his ticket in his hand.

4 Rewrite the sentences using the words in brackets.

a) The plan was for us to spend five days visiting the sights, but I was too ill to travel.
We were (supposed to) spend five days visiting the sights, but I was too ill to travel.

b) I was about to win the contract when suddenly the company backed out.
I (on the verge of) winning the contract when suddenly the company backed out

c) The show was meant to start on Tuesday but they postponed the opening night.
The show was (due to) start on Tuesday but they postponed the opening night.

d) We had imagined that it was going to be very difficult to find accommodation, but in fact, it was incredibly easy.
it (would) be very difficult to find accommodation but in fact, it was incredibly easy.

e) They had planned to catch the midday ferry, but they got caught up in traffic and missed it.
They were (going to) catch the midday ferry, but they got caught up in traffic and missed it.

f) The original plan was that the Queen would was to visit the hospital but there was a nurses' strike and she had to cancel.
(be to) _____

g) She had planned to go on holiday over Christmas, but she was too busy at work and had to postpone it.
She (supposed to) go on _____

h) I was so nervous I was about to call the whole thing off, but in the end I plucked up courage and walked on to the stage.
I was (on the verge of) calling _____

Vocabulary

1 Match a word from column A with a word from column B to make compound adjectives. Then use these combinations to complete the sentences below.

A		B	
a)	record- 6	1	moving
b)	smartly- 4	2	consuming
c)	slow- 1	3	skinned
d)	good- 7	4	dressed
e)	time- 2	5	spoken
f)	softly- 5	6	breaking
g)	hand- 8	7	looking
h)	fair- 3	8	painted

a) His clothes were quite formal. He was _smartly-dressed_ in a dark blue silk suit and a tie.

b) He was a very _good-looking_ man and, as soon as Becky saw him, she remarked on how handsome he was.

c) I could hardly hear a word she said. She was very _softly-spoken_ and I had to ask her several times to speak up.

d) She was very _fair-skinned_. It looked like she'd never been in the sun in her life.

e) I nearly gave up the course. I had to go to class three times a week and it took over an hour to get there. It was very _time-consuming_ and left me very little free time.

f) The traffic is very _slow-moving_ and on some parts of the motorway it's at a standstill.

g) Once the pots were taken out of the furnace they were _hand-painted_ by local artists.

h) It was a _record-breaking_ performance. He finished the race five seconds faster than the previous best time.

2 Complete the sentences with an appropriate compound adjective.

Example
These jeans were great value, they've lasted much longer than any other pair I've ever had.

They're a very *long-lasting* pair of jeans.

a) He just loves going out and having fun.
   He's a _fun-loving_ kind of person.

b) She always behaves really badly in class.
   She's a _badly-behaved_ little girl.

c) He's very distinguished, tall and slim with grey hair.
   He's a tall, slim, _grey-haired_ gentleman.

d) The bread was delicious, made with tomatoes that had been left out to dry in the sun.
   The bread was made with _sun-dried_ tomatoes.

e) He works very hard and hardly ever takes a holiday.
   He's extremely _hard-working_.

f) His name must be foreign, it sounds very strange to my ear.
   He has a _strange-sounding_ name.

g) The children loved their present, a model car that they could operate with their voices.
   The children loved their present; a _voice-operated_ model car.

h) James wants to get a job in a country where Spanish is spoken.
   James wants to get a job in a _Spanish-speaking_ country.

3 Circle the correct preposition.

a) I really thought the film was going to be better than that. It didn't really live _up_ / on / at to my expectations.

b) She was amazed. There was so much to do before the inspection but they managed to pull it on / (off) / in without a single thing going wrong.

c) It rained non-stop all day and the pitch was completely waterlogged so finally they decided to call at / in / _off_ the match.

d) Nearly all the preparations had been done. Then suddenly the council decided not give us the licence to stage the concert and all our plans fell over / off / (through).

e) It was mayhem. Nobody knew what to do. There was a mix off / _up_ / on and my luggage ended up in Tokyo.

f) The lead singer had lost his voice and couldn't sing anymore, but the band decided to go at / up / _on_ with the concert so as not to disappoint their fans.

4 Replace the words in *italics* in each sentence with words from the box. Make any changes that are necessary.

fiasco	fell through	mix up	no-show

pull everything off   hitch   call off   go on
get your act together   live up to expectations

a) The whole thing was a complete *mess*. The bride was late and the best man forgot the ring. *fiasco*

b) We'll have to *cancel* the meeting until the director returns from Hong Kong. *call off*

c) I'm sorry that the deal *hasn't worked out*. Apparently they can't agree on the price. *has fallen through*

d) You're going to have to *be more organised*. If not, you may end up losing your job. *get your act together*

e) We were a little disappointed by the performance, the dancing *was not really up to the standard we'd been hoping for*. *didn't live up to our expectations*

f) I'm afraid the new network won't be ready for a week. We've come across a small *problem* with the design of the system. *hitch*

g) He doesn't think that she will be able *to make it all work*. I wish he had more faith in her. *pull everything off*

h) It turned out that the eclipse was a bit of a *disappointment*, as the clouds made it practically impossible to see anything. *no-show*

i) There's been some *confusion* with the plans. Ruth should be in London and Gavin should be visiting our client in Manchester. *mix up*

j) I don't know where he is but the show must *continue*; the audience is waiting. *go on*

Listening & reading

1 You are going to listen to a short story called *The Christmas Presents*. Cover the text and, as you listen, answer the following questions.

a) Who are the two main characters?

_____

_____

b) What Christmas presents did they buy for each other?

_____

_____

c) What sacrifices did they have to make to buy the presents?

_____

_____

The Christmas Presents

Della had been saving hard to buy a Christmas present for her husband, Jim, but it was Christmas Eve and the few cents she'd managed to scrape together weren't going to go very far.
(a) _____

As she stood in front of the mirror, her beautiful, long auburn hair hanging over her shoulders, she had an idea. She flung on her coat and her hat and marched out onto the street. She stopped in front of a door which bore a sign saying 'Hair Goods of All Kinds'. (b) _____
'Will you buy my hair?' asked Della.
'Let's have a look at it first,' said an old lady, turning to face Della.
Della took her hat off and let her thick, curly locks fall down her back.
'Twenty dollars. Will that do you?', asked the old lady. Della nodded dumbly, fighting back the tears as the first lock fell to the floor. (c) _____

She knew exactly what she was looking for. The one possession that Jim prized above all others was a gold watch that had been his father's and his grandfather's before him. The present that Della wanted to buy for him was a simple gold chain to hold this precious watch (d) _____ . She handed over the twenty dollars, wrapped the chain up safely in a piece of coloured tissue paper and set off for home.

On her way she stopped to look in the window of her favourite shop. It sold antique knick-knacks; earrings, rings and, there at the front of the window lay her favourites, a set of beautiful tortoiseshell hair combs. She and Jim had stopped here the other day to admire them. He'd run his fingers through her hair and told her that the combs would have looked beautiful against the dark red of her hair. He loved her hair almost as much as his watch. Della caught a glimpse of her reflection in the window and put her hand up to her newly-cut locks. What would Jim say? She was sure he'd forgive her once he saw his present. (e) _____

That evening as she waited for Jim to come home she felt excited, and a little apprehensive. When she heard his footsteps on the stairs, she ran to the door. (f) _____ His face crumpled and he reached out his hand, saying 'Your hair'.

She ran towards him, crying and apologising, (g) _____ and she thrust the tiny tissue paper parcel in his hand. He, at the same time, reached into his pocket and held out a small parcel of about the same size.
'My darling, of course I love you, with or without your hair, it's just that I bought these for you ...'
They both took the small, simply wrapped presents

from each other's trembling hands. Della bent over hers, hardly wanting to open it. There in her hand lay the tortoiseshell combs.

'Oh, my love,' she whispered, 'they're beautiful, so beautiful, but don't worry, my hair'll grow. This time next year I'll be wearing them, you'll see. Go on open your present ...'

His hands fumbled on the paper as he pulled out the gold chain, and his mouth shaped itself into a sad smile.

'Don't you like it?' she asked anxiously.

'It's perfect,' he said. 'But it's just that ... I sold my watch this evening ... to buy the combs!'

(h) _____ Jim drew Della towards him, kissed her gently on her short curls and said, 'Thank you. Thank you for the best present I could ever have.'

2 The story above is slightly shorter than the recorded version. Some descriptive phrases have been left out and numbers added in their place. Match the phrases from the box to the correct position in the text.

1 'Jim, I'm sorry, I'm sorry, but surely you still love me, don't you? I sold it. I sold it to buy you a present. Look!'

2 She summoned up her courage, pushed the door open and walked in.

3 The look on his face when he saw her was a hundred times worse than anything she could have expected.

4 The two looked at each other for a moment, not knowing whether to laugh or cry.

5 But once she had the money in her hand, the smile returned to her face and she skipped out of the shop to find a present for her beloved Jim.

6 She so wanted to get him something special, something that he would treasure.

7 And anyway, she thought her hair looked quite good in its new, boyish style.

8 ... for much as he loved it, he was still a little ashamed of using it in public because of the old leather strap he was forced to use in place of a chain.

[cassette icon] Listen again and check your answers.

3 Look back at the text and find words that mean:

a) collect or gather _____

b) dark red _____

c) walked determinedly _____

d) without speaking _____

e) a piece of hair _____

f) valued greatly _____

g) small objects _____

h) a quick look _____

i) nervous _____

j) moved clumsily _____

4 Complete the following sentences with words in 3. Make any changes that are necessary.

a) She kept a _____ of his hair hidden away between the pages of her book.

b) She _____ about £150 by doing various odd jobs during her spare time.

c) He woke everyone up, _____ around in the dark, bumping into the furniture and making a lot of noise.

d) She _____ up to the desk and demanded to speak to the manager.

e) I don't really like flying and I always feel a little bit _____ before I get on a plane.

f) When she heard the news, she just shook her head _____ , not knowing what to say.

5 Match these features of good story writing in box A to the extracts from the story in box B.

A

a) Keeps back important information until the end

b) Introduces the situation and the main characters at the very beginning.

c) Uses repetition to add emphasis

d) Reports thoughts

e) Uses direct speech

f) Adds descriptive details to noun phrases

g) Uses descriptive verbs

B

1 Della had been saving hard to buy a Christmas present for her husband, Jim.

2 She so wanted to get him something special, something that he would treasure.

3 She flung on her coat and her hat and marched out onto the street.

4 'Twenty dollars. Will that do you?', asked the old lady.

5 What would Jim say? She was sure he'd forgive her once he saw his present. And anyway, she thought her hair looked quite good in its new, boyish style.

6 They both took the small, simply wrapped presents from each other's trembling hands.

7 But it's just that... I sold my watch this evening... to buy the combs!

Writing

1 Look at a summary of another short story by O. Henry. Put the paragraphs in the correct order.

A Service of Love – O. Henry

a) They successfully keep up their lies until one day when Delia burns her hand. The girls in the laundry send down to the boiler room for a rag and some oil to put on her burn and she goes home with her hand bandaged up. She tells Joe a lie about how her hand was injured, (a) _____ he recognises the rags and gently teases a confession from her. He (b) _____ confesses his secret and they forgive each other, understanding that their love is far more important than their art.

b) Two young would-be artists move from the country to study in New York. Joe wants to become a painter, Delia a concert pianist. They meet in New York, fall in love and get married. They have high hopes and great ambitions (c) _____ . But, (d) _____ , their small town talents aren't good enough to bring them fame and fortune in the big city and very soon their money runs out. ☐

c) They both secretly realise that they will never become great artists, but they still believe in their partner's abilities, so they (e) _____ decide to get a job. (f) _____ , in order not to disappoint each other, they lie about their jobs, pretending that they are using their art to make money. Delia says she's giving piano classes to the daughter of a rich family, (g) _____ Joe says he's selling sketches to a rich patron. Delia is, (h) _____ , ironing shirts in a laundry and Joe is working in the boiler room of the very same laundry. ☐

2 Where would you expect to see this summary:

a) on the back cover of an anthology of his stories?
b) in an essay on one of O. Henry's short stories?
c) in a short newspaper review of a new anthology of his works?

3 Complete the summary with words from the box.

> in fact   for each other   too   unfortunately
> however   but   while   both

4 Which paragraph describes:

a) the surprise twist?   ☐
b) the basic problem?   ☐
c) the main characters?   ☐
d) the moral of the story?   ☐
e) their current situation?   ☐
f) their secret solutions?   ☐

5 Which of the following features are present in the summary:

a) Short, balanced sentences.
b) Keeping back important information until the end.
c) Use of narrative tenses (past simple, past continuous, past perfect)
d) Use of simple, clear discourse markers
e) Detailed descriptions of people, places and events.
f) Use of present tenses to narrate a story.

6 You are going to write a short summary of *The Christmas Presents* for the introduction to a new school anthology of O. Henry's short stories. Use the following paragraph plan to guide you. Read the story again, make notes on the information you are going to include and write the summary. You should write no more than 250 words.

Paragraph 1
Introduce the main characters and explain the basic situation and the problem they are both facing.

Paragraph 2
Explain what presents they want to buy for each other and why.

Paragraph 3
Explain the sacrifices they make to buy the presents and their reactions when they exchange gifts.

12 Words

Word quiz

The use of the prefix *tele* is very popular in the English language and rapidly growing. It comes from ancient Greek and means 'far'.

Choose the correct definition for the following *tele* words.

1   Telebroking means

   a)   buying and selling televisions

   b)   buying and selling stocks and shares by telephone

   c)   buying and selling stocks and shares in the telecommunications industry

2   Telegenic means

   a)   a television which also functions as a computer screen

   b)   a television personality who is famous for being an intellectual

   c)   having an appearance or manner that looks good on TV

3   Telecottage means

   a)   a special cyber cafe with office space that can be rented by the hour

   b)   a small house far away from any towns or villages

   c)   a house which is equipped with all the latest hi-tech gadgets

4   Telethon means

   a)   a series of marathon races run over a short period of time

   b)   an enormous television set used for screening football matches in public

   c)   a very long television programme, especially to raise money for charity

5   Telepresence means

   a)   the use of virtual reality technology to give the appearance of participating in distant events

   b)   the ability to make a big impact on television

   c)   electrical goods sold at discount prices

Grammar

1   Complete the text with *however, whatever, whenever, wherever, whoever* or *whichever*.

Shakespeare's work has been translated into hundreds of languages and you can find examples of it (a) _____ you go in the world. (b) _____ you think of his work, Shakespeare certainly had a way with words. Many argue that he is the most prolific writer of all time, the extent of his vocabulary and the inventiveness with which he wrote make him second to none.

(c) _____ I show friends around London I always take them to the Globe Theatre. It's really special and (d) _____ you take there will be fascinated by the place. Sitting on the south bank of the Thames, the theatre was reconstructed as close to the original as possible and the pub that Shakespeare stayed at (e) _____ he was in London is about 50 metres away and still exists today.

(f) _____ little interest you may have in the theatre generally, you can't help but be moved by the way in which Shakespeare represents our deepest emotions and this is all the more remarkable when you consider that Shakespeare's life was actually very conservative.

So (g) _____ you do while you are in London, go down to the Globe Theatre. There are always plays on and (h) _____ play you get to see, you'll leave wondering how one man's words can come so near to describing our deepest passions and emotions.

2 Rewrite the sentences using the words in the box.

whoever   whichever   whenever   however
wherever   whatever

a) I don't care what you do, as long as you don't tell him about our plans for his party.

_____

_____

b) It never seems to matter where I go on holiday, I always get ill.

_____

_____

c) No matter what time it is, when I go into the boss's office she's always in a bad mood.

_____

_____

d) The last person to leave has to check that the windows are locked.

_____

_____

e) Whether we take the coast road or the mountain road, we're going to be late.

_____

_____

f) It doesn't matter how long it takes, I'm going to finish this report before I go to bed.

_____

_____

HW.

3 Circle the correct verb.

a) He really is very funny. He had everyone *laugh / laughing* at dinner with his stories.

b) We had someone *come* / *coming* round straightaway to fix the car.

c) A: Are you sure you filled your tax form in correctly?

B: Yes, I had my accountant *check* / *checking* it for me before I sent it off.

d) The poor restaurant service and the awful food had everyone *complain / complaining* for the rest of the holiday.

e) A: Oh, Julia, you look absolutely stunning. Where did you get that dress?

B: I had Stella McCartney *make / making* it especially for the occasion.

f) The exam results had him *jump / jumping* for joy. He never imagined he would get top marks.

HW

4 Complete the letter using *have* in the correct form and the verbs in brackets.

Dear Anthea

How are you? Sorry we couldn't make your party last Saturday. We'd already organised to <u>have friends come over</u> (friends / come over) that weekend. They're actually in a band and later on in the evening they started playing some music and (a) _____ (everyone / dance). The problem was that we made so much noise that we (b) _____ (the neighbours / knock) on the door at three o'clock in the morning!

We're hoping to start the decorating in the next couple of weeks. We could do it ourselves but in the end we've decided that we'd rather (c) _____ (an expert / do) it.

However, before they do, Bill and I want to have a party and we'd love you to come along. We're going to (d) _____ (caterers / do) the food and drink so we'll be able to spend more time with everyone and actually get to enjoy our own party for a change.

Anyway, got to go. I'm looking after my sister's kids at the moment and they (e) _____ (me / run around) playing all kinds of games.

Hope to see you all soon.

Love
Vicky

Vocabulary

1 Complete the sentences with words or phrases from the box.

gap year   scratch card   retail therapy
spin doctor   semi-skimmed   quality time

a) I don't like milk that has too much fat so I always use _semi-skimmed_

b) When I'm feeling depressed I tend to go shopping and indulge in a bit of _retail therapy_

c) He's gambling-mad. He spends a fortune on the lottery and he always buys a _scratch card_ every time he goes shopping.

d) The government needed to repair their image with the public so they hired a _spin doctor_ to give them some advice.

e) Both of us work and so we spend very little _quality time_ with our children.

f) She's decided to take a *gap year* before going to university. She wants to do voluntary work in India.

2 Put these words in the correct order to make common phrases.

a) have my you word _____

b) me fail words _____

c) few man words a of _____

d) a in word _____

e) mouth word of _____

f) words in other _____

g) take for word it your I'll _____

h) into put it's words difficult to _____
_____

3 Complete these dialogues with some of the phrases in 2.

a) A: How do you publicise your courses?
B: We put adverts in the local newspaper and on the local radio, but it's mainly by _____ .

b) A: So what did you say?
B: Well, I told him I'd had enough and that I just wasn't going to stand for it anymore.
A: So, _____ , you told him you were leaving?

c) A: Tom's not very talkative today, is he?
B: Ah, well, you know him. He's _____ .

d) A: Don't tell anyone about this, will you?
B: Of course I won't. _____ !
A: Thanks, I know I can trust you on this.

e) A: This soup tastes really horrible! Do you want to try some?
B: No thanks! I think _____ and go for the salad instead.

f) A: Well, I just don't know what to say!
_____
B: Yes, I'm sorry, I know I should have told you sooner.

4 Complete the following texts with the words and phrases from the box.

addressing   recipient   signing off   dictates
get straight to the point   snail mail

If you want to congratulate someone on getting a new job, buying a new house, or on their recent engagement, e-greetings can be the perfect

solution, especially if speed (a) _____ your choice. There's a number of great websites that offer a range of different e-cards. As well as being much faster than sending a message by (b) _____ , e-greetings also allow us to add music or animation and to personalise the greeting to suit the (c) _____ and the occasion.

If you are answering a request for information by e-mail you need to follow the usual conventions of letter-writing; (d) _____ the reader formally, using 'Dear Mr / Ms' and the person's surname, and (e) _____ formally as well, using formulas such as 'Yours sincerely' or 'Best regards'. Remember to keep your message short and make sure you (f) _____ and don't waste time your reader's time or try their patience.

Pronunciation

1 Circle all the silent consonants in these sentences.

a) He knelt down and asked Fiona if she would marry him.

b) He was living in Cambridge, studying Psychology before becoming a journalist.

c) There was no doubt in her mind about the importance of leaving right now.

d) They built a huge sign advertising the opening of the bar.

e) She knows when she leaves university she might have quite a large debt with the bank.

f) If he doesn't agree with the party's social policies, he really should resign.

[▪▪] Listen to check your answers.

2 Put the words in the box into three groups according to their vowel sounds.

trouble   they   blind   great   high   enough
page   write   cup   does   eight   either
blood   buy   rain

/aɪ/ d<u>ie</u>   /eɪ/ r<u>a</u>dio   /ʌ/ m<u>o</u>ther

_____   _____   _____

_____   _____   _____

_____   _____   _____

_____   _____   _____

_____   _____   _____

[▪▪] Listen to check your answers.

3 Which is the odd one out in these groups of words?

a) prefer church clerk work journey learn

b) heart aunt laugh artist machine half

c) through one clue juice soup chew

d) eat police field receive key friend

e) because dead any said bury leisure

f) clock watch daughter quantity sausage knowledge

🔲 Listen to check your answers.

Listening & reading

1 🔲 You are going to listen to a short extract from a radio programme called *Job Hunt*. (If you don't have the recording, read the tapescript on page 79.) As you listen answer the questions:

a) Who is the programme aimed at? _____

b) Who is the guest speaker? What does she do? _____

c) Which of the following topics do they speak about? _____

- Writing CVs. ☐
- Writing cover letters. ☐
- Attending a job interview. ☐
- Applying for jobs by e-mail. ☐
- Filling in application forms. ☐

d) Where can listeners find out more about the topic?

2 Read the following statements and decide if they are true (T) or false (F).

a) A cover letter can replace a CV. ☐

b) A cover letter is important as it can help you create a good first impression. ☐

c) You should repeat the main points from your CV in the letter. ☐

d) It should be impersonal and factual. ☐

e) E-mail and Internet have made recruitment more efficient. ☐

f) E-mail cover letters are shorter and less formal than traditional cover letters. ☐

🔲 Listen again to check your answers.

3 Complete the expressions below with the verbs from the box.

add give take do (2) make (x3)

a) _____ a personal touch

b) _____ (someone) a favour

c) _____ your best

d) _____ (someone) a chance

e) _____ a difference

f) _____ an effort

g) _____ a good impression

h) _____ your time

4 Complete the following extracts from the radio programme with the expressions in 3. Make any changes that are necessary.

a) A cover letter is a short letter of introduction written to accompany your CV. It's often the first contact you have with a potential employer and it's your first chance to _____ .

b) … it can often _____ between getting an interview or having your CV ignored.

c) It _____ to demonstrate your written communication skills.

d) Just as you would _____ to look smart and professional for a job interview, …

e) … so you should _____ to make as good a first visual impression as possible with your cover letter.

f) It really is important to _____ over it, don't rush it, and make sure to double check it for spelling mistakes …

g) … always ask someone to _____ of reading over it for you before you send it off. It's always easier for an objective eye to spot mistakes or discrepancies.

h) It is there to interpret the factual information included in your CV and to

_____ .

Check your answers in the tapescript on page 79.

5 Read this article about common errors made when writing cover letters.

Top Five Cover Letter Blunders

There are certain errors that promise to diminish your hard work of writing a cover letter. From typographical mishaps to erroneous employer information, all mistakes have a negative impact on the application process. Serious errors will land your application in the wastebasket. Be forewarned: carefully read your cover letter at least twice. The following list outlines some of the most common cover letter mistakes and, more importantly, suggests ways to correct them.

a) _____

Tailor your cover letter to the specific position applied for. Your letter should convey a genuine interest in the position and a long-term pledge to fulfilling its duties. For example, I am very interested in this proof reading position, and I am confident in my ability to make a long term contribution to your company.

b) _____

Since cover letters are generally short, every word of every sentence should be directly related to your purpose for writing. Any other information weakens your application. For example, mentioning that you are a certified gymnastic instructor while applying for the post of civil engineer.

c) _____

Do not include your age, weight, height, marital status, race, religion, or any other personal information unless you feel that it directly pertains to the position that you're seeking. For instance, height and weight may be important if you are applying to an athletic team. Similarly, you should list your personal interests and hobbies only if they are directly relevant to the type of job you are seeking. If you are applying to a company that greatly values teamwork, for instance, citing that you organised a community fund-raiser or played on a basketball team will probably be advantageous. When in doubt, however, leave it out.

d) _____

Although some applicants might choose the third person ('he' or 'she') as a creative approach to presenting their qualifications, potential employers sometimes find this voice disconcerting. In general, using the first person voice is preferable.

e) _____

It is very easy to make mistakes in your letters, particularly when you are writing many in succession. But it is also very easy for a recruitment manager to reject out of hand any cover letter that contains errors, even those that seem minor at first glance. Here are a few common technical mistakes to watch out for when proof reading your letter:

• Misspelling the recruitment manager's name or title in the address, in the greeting, or on the envelope.
• Forgetting to change the name of the organisation you're applying to each time it appears in your application, especially in the body of the letter.
• Indicating application for one position and mentioning a different position in the body of the letter.

Now put the paragraph titles in the correct place in the text.

1 Choice of Pronouns
2 Focus on the Particular Job
3 Typographic Errors
4 Unnecessary Career Information
5 Irrelevant Personal Information

Writing

1 Look at this checklist of things to remember when writing an e-mail cover letter for a job. Put a tick (✓) for the Dos and a cross (✗) for the Don'ts.

a) avoid using paragraphs to separate the sections of your letter   **✗**
b) use contracted forms or abbreviations
c) be as polite as you would if you were meeting the person for the first time
d) include irrelevant information
e) use a spell check and proof read your letter carefully
f) use the subject line to explain why you are writing
g) duplicate information included in your CV
h) attach a CV in a separate document
i) leave the recipient's name out and avoid signing off as in a normal letter
j) be too chatty or informal as you would in an e-mail to a friend
k) explain which post you are applying for
l) keep it brief and to the point

2 Read this e-mail cover letter and answer the following questions:

a) What position is the person applying for?
b) What points on the checklist has he forgotten?

From: Robbie To: staffing@dunroe.co.uk
Subject: re. post of freelance translator
attachment: Robbie's CV

I'm writing to apply fro the post of freelance translator advertised in the Guardian on February 27th. I graduated in English and Europaen Studies at the University of Naples in 1996. After graduating I worked for six months as a trainee in a local trade journal but decided that I didn't like the job and left to study for my translator exams. I passed these in June 1997 and then wnet on to work for a series of small translation agencies in my home town.

I am currently looking for a more permanent position which will allow me to improve my skills and develop as a translator. I think your company will benefit form my experience and my abilities. I am available for interview any time next week.

That's all for now,
Robbie

3 Underline the phrases Robbie uses to explain

a) why he's writing
b) why he is interested in the post
c) what he has to offer
d) when he can attend an interview

4 Look at the job advert below and answer the following questions:

a) What is the position?
b) What are the minimum requirements?
c) What other qualifications and/or experience would be helpful.

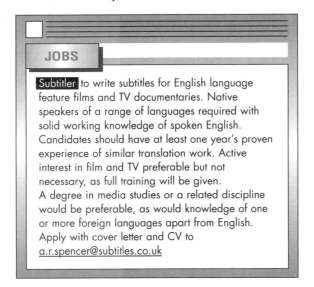

JOBS

Subtitler to write subtitles for English language feature films and TV documentaries. Native speakers of a range of languages required with solid working knowledge of spoken English. Candidates should have at least one year's proven experience of similar translation work. Active interest in film and TV preferable but not necessary, as full training will be given. A degree in media studies or a related discipline would be preferable, as would knowledge of one or more foreign languages apart from English. Apply with cover letter and CV to a.r.spencer@subtitles.co.uk

5 You are going to apply for the job. Write a cover letter to accompany your CV. Invent any information you need to. Use the format below to help you. You should write approximately 250 words.

Dear Mr/Ms Last Name, (If you don't know their name: Dear Sir or Madam,)

First Paragraph:
Why You Are Writing. Remember to make a clear reference to the post you are applying for.

Middle Paragraphs:
1 Why You Are Interested. Remember to include a short description of your current work position.

2 What You Have to Offer. Convince the readers that you are a suitable candidate and that they should call you for interview. Make connections between your abilities and the job requirements in the advert.

Final Paragraph:
Your Availability. Remember to let the readers know when you are available for interview and how best to get in touch with you. Include a phone number and times when you can be reached on it.

Yours sincerely, (or 'Yours faithfully' if you don't know the person's name)

Your Typed Name

13 Conscience

Quotes

Reorder the words in the quotations below.

a) that warns you / the inner voice / might be looking / conscience is / that someone
   (H.L. Mencken)

b) a short memory / for / a lot of people / mistake / a clear conscience
   (Doug Larson)

c) hurts / a conscience / everything else / when / is what / feels good
   (Anon)

Grammar

1 Match the sentences in box A to the correct reply in box B.

A

4	a)	I really am fed up with always putting my hand in my pocket.
3	b)	We're running a bit late.
7	c)	She is really tired and needs a break.
5	d)	My car keeps breaking down.
1	e)	His exam results are getting worse.
2	f)	John really hasn't got the experience to run the project.
6	g)	I don't agree with giving money to charities.

B

1   I wish I could spend more time with him to help him with his studies.

2   I'd rather we recruited someone with more of a background in this area.

3   I think it's time we made a move.

4   It's high time he learnt to pay his own way.

5   If only I had the money to buy a new one.

6   I'd rather people volunteered some of their time.

7   It's time she had a holiday.

2 Correct the mistakes in these sentences.

a) I'm getting really unfit. I think it's time I ~~join~~ *joined* a gym

b) She'd rather ~~spent~~ *spend* the weekend in a quiet country village than in a busy city.

c) I wish I ~~don't~~ *didn't* have to work today. I'm feeling really tired.

d) If only there ~~wouldn't~~ *wasn't* be so much bureaucracy involved in charity work perhaps then the charities would be able to get things done more quickly.

e) She wishes she ~~can~~ *could* come with us on holiday but her work commitments are going to keep her at home.

f) I'd rather you ~~not~~ *didn't* do that. It might be dangerous.

g) It really is high time the government ~~would do~~ *did* something more concrete to help the homeless.

h) He said he'd rather I ~~might~~ *gave* give the presentation, as I've done it before and I know what's needed.

3 Rewrite the second sentence so that it means the same as the first.

a) I really think the local authorities should do something about the traffic.
   It's high time _the local authorities did something about the traffic_ ,

b) Please don't smoke in my car.
   I'd rather _you didn't smoke in my car_ .

c) I would like to see more of my wife, but I can't because she works at weekends.
   I wish _I could see more of my wife, but I can't because she works at weekends_ ,

d) I really regret not having done something to help raise money for charity when I was a student.
   I wish _I had done some something to help raise money for charity when I was a student,_

e) I think someone needs to teach him a few manners. He's very rude.
   It's high time _someone needed to teach him a few manners, He's very rude_

f) I really think he should stop wasting time and settle down to a good job.
It's about time *he stopped wasting time and settle down to a good job.*

g) I'd prefer you to stay at home and look after the children so that I can go shopping.
I'd rather *you stayed at home and look after the children so that I can go shopping.*

Vocabulary

1 Put the words in the correct order.

a) a / idea / I / rather / it / strange / thought / was
It was rather a strange idea I thought.

b) would / me / did / rather / I / than / you / it
I would rather you did it than me.

c) it / rather / she / was / that / say / silly / to / thought / thing / a

d) ghost / looked / white / her / rather / powdered / with / a / face / she / like
She rather looked like a ghost with her white powdered face

e) about / better / be / depressed / it's / rather / to / get / than / positive / it
It rather be positive ...... to get better than it is about depressed

f) school / Tom / you / or / know / do / the studies / college / rather / where / the / ?
Do you know the school, or rather the college, where Tom studies?

g) not / I'd / to / last / really / have / party / night / gone / rather / the
I'd rather really not have gone to the party last night.

h) a / you / bungee / to / going / do / are / really / jump / ? / than / me / rather / you / !
Are you going to a bungee jump? Rather you than me!

2 Rewrite these sentences using *rather*. Make any necessary changes.

a) I'm feeling quite tired after a long day at work.
I'm feeling rather tired after a long day at work.

b) I think I'd prefer to go away for the weekend than stay at home.
I think I'd rather go away for the weekend than stay at home.

c) He's just started a new job, or should I say, he's been offered one.
He's just started a new job, or rather, he's been offered one

d) Catherine looks quite a lot like her mother when her mother was her age.
Catherine looks rather like her mother when her mother was her age.

e) I'd prefer not to go on holiday with your parents.
I'd rather not go on holiday with your parents.

3 Circle the correct word in the sentences below.

a) You see a lot of people *collecting* / *getting* / *putting* money for charity.

b) Though there is no money involved, a lot of people like working for charities because it makes them feel good *with* / *about* / *of* themselves.

c) She did a parachute jump to *earn* / *gain* / *raise* money for a local charity.

d) I got people to *sponsor* / *give* / *invest* me for every length of the pool I swam.

e) It really was a big *performance* / *event* / *spectacle* and included a concert, a dinner and an enormous fireworks display.

f) He went round door *at* / *to* / *in* door putting leaflets in people's letterboxes about the forthcoming charity function.

g) The most important thing is that the charity gets a high *profile* / *publicity* / *image*.

h) We managed to get a few *TV workers* / *celebrities* / *volunteers* to come and support the show and that created a lot of publicity.

4 Complete these words with the missing vowels.

a) p o v e rty   str i ck e n

b) h u m a n   r i ghts

c) c a mp a i gns

d) b o yc o tts

e) i ss u e

f) l i v e l i h o o d

g) i mp a ct

h) h a b i t a t

5 Complete the following sentences with the words in 4.

a) The main _____ issue _____ being discussed was whether to allow tobacco companies to sponsor the event.

b) First Aid charities such as the Red Cross not only offer help in war zones but also help out in _____ poverty stricken _____ areas.

c) A lot of charities organise _____ boycotts _____ against products, encouraging consumers not to buy them.

d) The United Nations declaration of _____ human rights _____ states that all children have the right to primary education.

e) The Worldwide Fund for Nature is fighting to save the natural _____ habitat _____ of the giant panda from being destroyed.

f) Some charity _____ campaigns _____ have an incredible _____ impact _____ and really affect people emotionally.

g) The _____ livelihood _____ of many people in developing countries depends on the support and help that charities provide.

6 Complete these sentences with words from the box.

> my an on guilty her a in clear
> easy all ease a

a) You can say what you like. But I know I didn't have anything to do with it. I've got _____ a clear _____ conscience. = don't feel guilty

b) I can't see how she'll ever forget the incident. It'll be _____ a guilty _____ conscience forever. She knows that she is partly responsible.

c) _____ In all _____ = without feeling guilty conscience, can you really say that when you see people begging for money on the street, you don't feel bad?

d) Thanks for popping in and checking on my grandmother. It helps _____ ease _____ my = clear your conscience. I'm worried about leaving her on mind her own.

e) Don't worry. Our company will look after all the arrangements so that you can enjoy the day with _____ an easy _____ conscience.

f) She's suffering from _____ on her _____ remember sth + feel conscience. She knows it was her fault and guilty feels terrible. about it.

Pronunciation

1 Look at the questions and answers below. Underline the word that is stressed in each of the questions.

a) 1 A: Did you enjoy your holiday?
   B: Yes, I did. It was great.

   2 A: Did you enjoy your holiday?
   B: Yes, but my brother hated every minute of it!

b) 1 A: Are you doing the fun run?
   B: No, I'm competing in the women's half marathon.

   2 A: Are you doing the fun run?
   B: No, I hate running! But Jim's doing it if you want to sponsor him.

▭ Listen to check your answers.

2 Read these short dialogues and underline the main stress or stresses in each sentence.

a) A: So, you went out with Darren last night, did you?

   B: No, I went out with Keith, his twin brother.

b) A: Did you enjoy the show? Tom didn't think it was that good.

   B: Yes, I did. I thought it was great, but Jane thought it was really awful.

c) A: Tim told me you were thinking of going to the beach this weekend.

   B: No, nothing's changed, we're still going the weekend after next.

d) A: So, how much money did you make?
   B: About five hundred pounds, I think. I raised about twenty five.

▭ Listen to check your answers.

Reading & listening

1 Look at the flyer on page 72 for a charity called *Comic Relief* and answer these questions.

a) What are *Comic Relief's* main objectives?
   _____

b) How do they fulfil these objectives?
   _____

c) Where does the money go?
   _____

d) How much of the money they raise actually goes to charity?
   _____

COMIC RELIEF

Why does *Comic Relief* exist?

Comic Relief is seriously committed to helping end poverty and social injustice in the UK and the poorest countries in the world.

We do this by:

- **raising** money from the general public by actively involving them in events and projects that are innovative and fun.

- **informing**, educating, raising awareness and promoting social change.

- **allocating** the funds we raise in a responsible and effective way to a wide range of charities which we select after careful research.

- **ensuring** that our Red Nose Day fundraising costs are covered by sponsorship in cash or in kind so that *every penny raised goes to charity.*

2 🔲 Listen to a radio interview with Janet Whittal, a volunteer worker for Comic Relief. Then answer these questions.

a) When was the charity founded?

_____

b) Why was it founded?

_____

c) Why is it called Comic Relief?

_____

d) What's the name of the main event organised by this charity?

_____

e) What sort of activities do the fund-raisers get involved in?

_____

f) What kind of people get involved?

_____

3 Which of these topics are *not* discussed?

a) the people who founded the charity ☐

b) the main difference between Comic Relief and other charity organisations ☐

c) the amount of money raised ☐

d) the projects funded by the charity ☐

e) the main fund-raising events ☐

f) the celebrities who support the cause ☐

🔲 Listen to the interview again to check.

4 Match words from column A with words from column B to form noun phrases from the interview. Then use these combinations to complete the sentences below.

A		B	
a)	wide	1	reversal
b)	organised	2	costumes
c)	good	3	events
d)	devastating	4	camp
e)	refugee	5	famine
f)	silly	6	cause
g)	active	7	audience
h)	role	8	part

a) At the time there was a

_____ in Sudan and

Ethiopia.

b) The charity was actually launched from a

_____ in Sudan.

c) But it isn't only a celebrity charity, is it? It does appeal to a very _____ .

d) The appeal of doing something silly in a

_____ is very powerful.

e) In 1997 more than 72% of the British population actually took an

_____ in the Biannual

Red Nose Day.

f) ... a lot of people love the sponsored

_____ events – bosses get sponsored to be a secretary or a receptionist for the day.

g) ... then of course there are the huge

_____ , like the Red Nose

Fun Run ...

h) ... with thousands of runners jogging through the City of London in various

_____ .

Writing

1 Read this flyer advertising a charity fund-raising event. The paragraphs are not in the correct order. Reorder them so that they match the paragraph headings.

The Grand Appeal
COMING YOUR WAY!

WALLACE AND GROMIT'S WRONG TROUSERS DAY

1 What is it?	a)	OK! Here's what you do. On Friday 7 July, with your friends and colleagues, go to work, or to the pub, or shopping or whatever dressed as you normally would down to the waist. But below the waist, let your imagination rip! Are you a city gent but secretly yearn to be Superman? Well your legs can be! Ever seen a secretary whose legs play for Man Utd? We have! And who was that builder in a tutu?!
2 How did it start?	b)	Great! We want two million people or more like you to bring a smile to the face of Britain. To take part get in touch with us at www.wrongtrousers@grandappeal.org.uk, or phone free phone 602 385 777. And remember, for the sake of children …
3 Interested?	c)	Wrong Trousers Day is a funky fun-filled festival of laughs that will help you to help children in hospital.
4 Still interested?	d)	The first festival took place in Bristol in 1997 in support of the Southwest's children's hospital. Every year since then nearly 200,000 men, women and children have cast off their inhibitions with their normal trousers or skirts to raise a fantastic £500,000! Now Wallace and Gromit want you to join the action and help children's hospitals and hospices in Newcastle, Sheffield, Manchester, Leicester, Nottingham and Cardiff as well as Bristol.

IT'S RIGHT TO BE WRONG

On Friday 7 July
WALLACE AND GROMIT'S WRONG TROUSERS DAY

2 Match the paragraphs to the following summaries:

1 a short description of the history behind the event and the cause it's raising money for ☐

2 details on what exactly the event involves ☐

3 details about how to get involved ☐

4 an introduction to the event ☐

3 Which of the following descriptions best describes the style of the flyer?

a) It is serious and informative, appealing to the reader's sense of fair play and social conscience by including facts and figures about the causes the charity supports.

b) It is fun and informative. It seems to be speaking directly to the reader. It uses questions, exclamations and adjectives very much as we would in speech.

c) It is fun and appeals to the reader's sense of humour, using jokes and rhymes to make its point. It does not however include any factual information about the charity or the event.

4 You are going to write a flyer for a similar fund-raising event. Follow the steps below:

a) Decide on the kind of event you are going to advertise. It should be fun and appeal to as many people as possible. It might be a fun run, a sponsored dance, a costume idea (such as the red nose or the wrong trousers), etc.

b) Decide what charity you are raising money for.

c) Think of a catchy slogan or name for your event.

d) Draw up a flyer using headings, sub-headings and short, clear paragraphs. Remember to use questions, exclamations and adjectives as in the model above.

You should write approximately 250 words.

14 Review 2

Grammar

1 Correct the mistakes in these sentences.

a) I hope I can get my brother to helping me *(help)* move house this weekend.

b) I'll have been finishing *(finished)* the painting by the time you come over to see us.

c) This time tomorrow I'm sitting *(will be sitting)* by the pool, relaxing with a drink in my hand.

d) Whoever *(Whenever)* you call me, I'll come and pick you up.

e) It really was frightening. The scene where the boy suddenly leaps out of the coffin had me *jumping* jump out of my seat.

f) Such disappointed *(so + adj.)* was he with his team's performance that he never renewed his season ticket.

g) They said they *(they'd)* check all the details before handing in the report.

h) By the end of the night the group really got going and had everybody dance. *dancing*

i) He can't missed *(have)* the train. Jean said she took him to the station and saw him get on it, so there must be some other explanation.

j) He neither enjoyed the holiday, nor he did try to hide it.

2 Rewrite these sentences using the words in brackets.

a) Whereas the law in England recognises different types of murder, US law only recognises one.
(however) *However,*

b) It's time we went, or we'll hit the rush hour.
(get) *got going,*

c) He speaks so quietly I can hardly hear what he's saying.
(softly-spoken) *He's so softly-spoken, I can hardly hear what he's saying.*

d) I persuaded John to come over to do the painting.
(get) *I got John to come over to do the painting.*

e) The problem with doing the decorating yourself is that it can take up a lot of time.
(time-consuming) *The problem with doing the decorating yourself is that it can be very time-consuming*

f) It doesn't matter what you have to do, just make sure you get it done before she gets home.
(Whatever) *you have to do just*
_____

g) He doesn't really get on with the neighbours and his wife doesn't either.
(neither) *neither does his wife.*

h) I'm sure he took the money. He was the only person in the room all evening.
(must) *He must have taken money*

i) The government hasn't attempted to resolve the issue with the dock workers and it hasn't made any plans for the imminent strike action.
(nor) *nor has it made any plans for the imminent strike action*

j) He was so determined to succeed that he paid little attention to those around him.
(such) *Such was his determined*

3 Complete the text with words and phrases from the box.

but then it's true that   however   after all
but   in this sense   also   whereas
but by then   more importantly   but now

ABBA was undoubtedly one of the greatest musical phenomena of the 20th century. The success of the group was mainly due to the joint songwriting talents of Benny Anderson and Bjorn Ulvaeus. They met at a party in 1966 and began writing songs together the following year.
(a) *However* , it wasn't until 1972 and after several failed attempts that the group that was to become known as ABBA was formed, releasing their first single *People Need Love*.

The name ABBA, which originated from the first letter of the names of each of the members of the group, wasn't used until 1973. Before that, they had called themselves 'Bjorn and Benny, Agnetha and Anni-Frid', which was a bit of a mouthful to say the least. The new name was actually the result of a newspaper competition (b) _____ *but* _____ before it could be used, permission had to be granted from a fish company that was already using the same name.

In 1973, at their second attempt, ABBA became the Swedish representatives for the Eurovision Song Contest. Their song won easily and, (c) _____ *more importantly* _____, within weeks their entry *Waterloo* was heading charts all over the world.

ABBA went on to release many more hit singles and international top-selling albums, and they (d) _____ *also* _____ made a full length feature film, *ABBA – The movie*. They produced their last single in December 1982, (e) _____ *but by then* _____ their success was beginning to wane. Curiously, in 1992 a massive revival carried them through into the next decade and the album *ABBA Gold* became their biggest selling album ever.

4 Circle the correct form of the verb.

Bill: Did you get that work (a) *finishing* / *finished* in the end?

Kate: No, I didn't. I know I really (b) *should* / *can* have, I mean I (c) *could* / *must* have worked all night on it ... but I just didn't have the energy.

Bill: Don't be silly! They surely (d) *mustn't* / *can't* have expected you to work all night!

Kate: I don't know, you'd be surprised! I really thought they (e) *ought* / *would* understand, but my boss was really angry when I said I (f) *would* / *will* need another day.

Bill: So what's going to happen then?

Kate: Well, they've given me until the end of the weekend to get it (g) *do* / *done*.

Bill: But you were (h) *on the verge of* / *going to* go away for the weekend!

Kate: I know, but it just looks like I (i) *'ll* / *'d* have to change my plans, doesn't it?

Bill: It's time you (j) *would stand* / *stood* up for yourself. They can't treat you like that!

Kate: If only I (k) *could!* / *can!* But I'd lose my job.

5 There is one word too many in each of the following sentences. What is it?

a) By the time we get home we'll have ~~been~~ seen most of the tourist spots in London.

b) Is that Debra's umbrella? She must ~~not~~ have forgotten it.

c) It's high time he ~~did~~ tried for a promotion; he's been with the company for at least five years.

d) I know I really should ~~to~~ have phoned you earlier, I hope I'm not disturbing you.

e) I was on the verge of ~~to~~ leaving the house when the phone rang.

f) They were supposed to ~~have~~ arrive at 10.30, I think.

g) Whichever ~~that~~ you choose, I hope you'll be very happy.

h) I'd rather not ~~to~~ have gone to the party, but I felt I had to.

Vocabulary

1 Match a word from column A with a word from column B to make compound nouns. Then use these combinations to complete the sentences below.

A		B	
a)	urban 3	1	doctor
b)	home 5	2	engine
c)	quality 8	3	myth
d)	first 7	4	sentence
e)	road 6	5	page
f)	search 2	6	rage
g)	spin 1	7	aid
h)	suspended 4	8	time

a) He didn't know where to find information about learning French on the Net so he used a _*search engine*_ to help him find the home page for the French Tourist Authority.

b) Luckily, when the accident happened there was someone there who had done a course in _*first aid*_ and was able to attend to the injured.

c) Now that he isn't working full-time he's able to spend more _*quality time*_ with his children.

d) The increase in traffic and stress related to driving has resulted in a massive increase in the incidents of _*road rage*_.

e) The judge decided not to send him to prison. Instead he gave him a _*suspended*_. *sentence*

f) The Prime Minister needs to improve his image and popularity, so he's employed a _spin doctor_ to help him do this.

g) The opening page of a website is often called the _home page_.

h) It's a great story, but I really don't think it's true. It sounds more like an _urban myth_ to me.

2 Which is the odd one out in the following groups of words?

a) trespassing graffiti vandalism arson (sue)

b) prominent prior to seeking (trick) _informal_ severe

c) altitude oxygen (pot-holing) summit ridges

d) hyperlink bookmark (newsgroup) inbox chat room

e) well-informed (time-consuming) comfort-loving softly-spoken newly-arrested

3 Complete these sentences with words from 2.

a) He's incredibly _well-informed_, he reads the paper from cover to cover every day in order to keep up with what's happening in the world.

b) He set fire to the building on purpose. He was later convicted of _arson_ and sent to prison for four years.

c) It was a real cyber-romance. They met in a _chat room_ and didn't actually see each other in the flesh until about four months later.

d) The paper wrote something about my client that wasn't true and my client now intends to _sue_.

e) When we reached the _summit_ we stood there in awe at the breath-taking view of the valleys below.

f) The police caught him writing all over the walls with a spray can again, but nothing will happen because _graffiti_ is a minor offence.

g) He tried to _trick_ the security guard into believing he was a member of the press in order to gain access to the building.

h) Designing my first webpage was fairly _time-consuming_, but it was worth it as I learnt a lot about html programming.

4 Complete these sentences with the correct form of the words in brackets.

a) One big advantage with e-mail is that you can also send _attachment_ such as photos. (attach)

b) His behaviour among other prison inmates was so bad that they decided to punish him with a week of solitary _confinement_. (confine)

c) The rate of _production_ of computer games has increased threefold over the last ten years. (produce)

d) The _accused_ was asked to stand while the judge read out the verdict. (accuse)

e) You need to be extremely well-_co-ordinated_ if you are going to learn to rock climb without the use of ropes. (co-ordinate)

f) Are you an _initiator_ or are you a follower? Do our quiz and find out! (initiate)

g) They had great _expectations_ for him and thought he would soon be ready to make a bid for the world record. (expect)

h) Remember that if you do not know the name of the _receiver_ of your letter, you should always start your letter with 'Dear Sir or Madam'. (receive)

i) More and more countries are banning _sponsorship_ deals with tobacco companies. (sponsor)

j) His _livelihood_ depended on the land he worked and he was very hard hit by the severe floods. (live)

5 Complete these sentences with the prepositions from the box.

up against down on in (x2) to (x2)

a) to be _in_ trouble with the law.

b) to lay _down_ the law.

c) to come up _against_ a problem.

d) to pluck _up_ the courage.

e) to live up __to__ expectations.

f) to have it __on__ your conscience.

g) to spring __to__ mind

h) to put your life __in__ danger

6 Complete these sentences with the phrases from 5. Make any changes that are necessary.

a) I heard that he ___was in trouble with the law___ again. I saw the police visiting his mother's house.

b) I really thought the show would be much better. It really didn't ___live up to my expectations___ .

c) We were looking for someone to take over the post of marketing director and your name just ___sprung to mind___. Would you be interested in applying?

d) He's always trying ___to lay down the law___ and tell me what I should do. He acts as if he was my boss.

e) I don't think I'll ever get over the fact that the car accident was my fault. I'll ___have it on my conscience___ for the rest of my life.

f) She was really worried about asking her boss for a pay rise but in the end she ___plucked up the courage___ .

g) Firemen are one of society's unsung heroes, they're constantly ___putting their lives in danger___ in order to save people's homes and possessions.

h) Everything was going fine when suddenly we ___came up against a problem___ and no one could find a solution.

Pronunciation

1 Read the short conversation below. The final *t* and *d* consonants are underlined. Circle the underlined *t*s and *d*s that are *not* pronounced.

Jeff: So, how di_d_ your interview go?

Rob: No_t_ too ba_d_, actually. They aske_d_ quite a few really difficul_t_ questions, bu_t_ luckily I'_d_ been studying har_d_ the nigh_t_ before and I coul_d_ answer all of them.

Jeff: So, when will they le_t_ you know abou_t_ the job?

Rob: They sai_d_ they'_d_ be in touch sometime nex_t_ week.

Jeff: Well, I really hope i_t_ goes well for you. You deserve i_t_.

Listen to check your answers.

2 Look at the list of words below. Underline the stressed syllable. The first one has been done for you.

ad<u>ven</u>ture

telepathy

therapy

production

quality

recipient

pioneer

photographer

transparent

suspended

Listen to check your answers.

3 Look at this list of words that are associated to the words in 3. Underline the stressed syllable and make a note as to whether the stressed syllable has moved or not.

ad<u>ven</u>turous   *no*

telepathic

therapeutic

productivity

qualitative

receipt

pioneering

photographic

transparency

suspension

Listen to the words being pronounced to check your answers.

Tapescripts

1 Identity

Interviewer Gary, you're a single father. Can you tell us something about your circumstances?

Gary Well, I split up from my wife and she had the kids at first but they came to live with me when she decided to move south because of work. I think Sara, the youngest, was about four and Gina was about ten. It didn't really seem like much of a change at first because I was used to them coming over at the weekends anyhow.

Interviewer So, I suppose you had to learn to cook, sew and iron.

Gary Hah no, not really, hah, I mean, well, I think that women fuss a lot. You know, they pay attention to detail. My attitude is get the job done, so I'm, I'm not a brilliant cook. I try to prepare stuff that's healthy but simple. You know, lots of pasta, fruit, salads and stuff. Sewing? Well, I haven't got a clue. Hah, I pay someone to do it. I suppose I do make an effort with the house, we keep it tidy and the kids help me anyway. I think that's one thing. My wife used to annoy me because anything I cleaned or washed was never good enough and so she would do it again. If the kids help me, I never say 'Oh, not like that'. I'm just pleased it's done. I don't want to spend my life cooking and cleaning.

Interviewer So do you think they have suffered?

Gary I don't think they've suffered, I just think they've lived a different life. You see, I decided I wasn't going to completely change my life. So it meant that the girls had to join in. I took them to football, I took them to rock festivals and we went on camping holidays or travelled across Europe together. My wife was always telling me I was being irresponsible, but they loved it, and I think they benefitted a lot.

Interviewer How?

Gary Well, they've seen a lot. We camped on the beach on an island in Greece for a week. I think Sara was about eight at the time. They've seen bands like Travis, U2 and the Corrs and they've been all over Europe.

Interviewer Don't you think that you were being a bit selfish? I mean, they probably liked other groups.

Gary No, that's part of the deal. I've been to see Robbie Williams, Britney Spears and even S Club 7. We don't just do what I want.

Interviewer All that must have cost you a lot of money?

Gary No, not really. Some people spend money on their houses and cars. I like going out and doing things and I love my kids to share it all with me. I drive an old van and my house is comfortable but it's not a palace. If I lived with a woman, I'd probably have had to spend all the money on the house. Women want everything to look nice; they want the curtains to match and stuff. I would rather spend the money on going up to London for the day, or going camping somewhere. I think that sometimes women are too organised, they take the fun out of life.

Interviewer Did you get a lot of support from your parents?

Gary Um, yes and no. I didn't really ask for it. Of course, if I need their help, they're there, but my children were included in most of the things I did when they were younger so I didn't need babysitters. Things have changed now of course. Sara is 13 and Gina is 19. We do still go to football together and we nearly always go out for an Indian meal on Friday nights.

Interviewer What about your own relationships. I mean, do you have a girlfriend?

Gary At the start it was odd. I would collect the children from school and the mums never spoke to me. Then one day I organised a party for Sara and I met a lot of the children's parents. W ... well, a lot of the single mums became my friends and they are always trying to find me girlfriends. So, at the moment I'm seeing Sara's best friend's mother's sister. Hah, hah, how's that for complicated?

5 Luck

Caroline Did you see that film that was on last night?

Adrian What film was that?

Caroline 'Waking Ned.'

Adrian Oh, yeah, I know the one ... no, I didn't see it – I was working ... but I've heard it's really good.

Caroline Yeah, it is ... absolutely hilarious ... it's based on a true story ...

Adrian Oh, yeah, what's it about then?

Caroline Well, basically it's everybody's classic daydream, you know, winning the lottery.

Adrian There's nothing new in that, is there?

Caroline No, except this story is set in a tiny old village, near the sea, in the Republic of Ireland, and it's ... it's not a straightforward lottery win, it's more of a lottery scam ...

Adrian A 'scam' you say? You mean like they produce a false ticket or something?

Caroline Not exactly ... you see, basically there are these two friends, Jackie and Michael, and they see this story in the newspaper about how someone from the village has won the big one on the Irish Lottery. So, they decide to track down the winner, befriend him or her, whoever they are and try and get them to share the jackpot. But it turns out that the winner, Ned Devine, has died. They find him dead in his bed, with the winning ticket in his hand, and it's all quite tragic 'cos after playing the lottery all his life when he actually does win he keels over and dies from the shock of it!

Adrian Hah, hah. So, I suppose that means the money goes to some long lost relative or something?

Caroline No, well the thing is that he hasn't got any relatives ... so, basically the money's going to go unclaimed.

Adrian Well, can't they just nick the ticket from him?

Caroline No, 'cos he wrote his name on the back of it. So, what they do is, they decide that one of them's going to pretend to be Ned and try and get the money that way. Things start getting really funny when the Lottery representative turns up from Dublin to check the claim, and there's this hilarious scene where Michael has to dress up as Ned, but then things get complicated, 'cos the representative is going to check Ned's story in the village ...

Adrian And so, I suppose everybody wants to get in on the Lottery win.

Caroline Exactly! And Jackie and Michael persuade the villagers to come in on the scam.

Adrian ... and of course that way everybody gets to share the winnings ...

Caroline But, of course, there's one person who finds out they can make more money for themselves by reporting the attempted scam to the authorities, and it really looks at one point as if Jackie and Michael are going to get caught and thrown into jail ...

Adrian But, of course, everything works out all right in the end.

Caroline Well, yeah, of course it does, they overcome all their difficulties, persuade the Lottery representative to hand over the money and have an enormous party to celebrate the occasion. The film ends with this superb scene of a group of the men from the village standing on the cliff top watching the sun come up and drinking a last toast to the memory of Ned Devine, the saviour of the village.

Adrian A feel good movie then?

Caroline Oh, yes, definitely, the kind of film that puts a smile on your face. Well worth seeing ...

6 Mind

Mark Well, I suppose my job is pretty stressful. All medical staff have pretty stressful jobs, but working in the Accident and Emergency department is particularly bad. We have to be ready to react quickly and efficiently, and often people's lives are at stake. Sometimes it can be really exhilarating, but it's also exhausting, both mentally and physically. I find it really difficult to unwind when I go home, I mean, I can't just go home and sit down and watch TV, or, or read a book, I'm too tense and get really fidgety. Some people find it's good to talk about their work – you know, go out for a couple of drinks after work and all that, but I don't. I prefer to get away from it, do some sport, maybe go running, go to the gym or play a game of squash. Squash is really good. You can thrash out all the pent-up stress and release all that tension and I find it really helps me just empty my mind and switch off ...

Kay I live about sixty miles away from where I work, and I commute in and out every day on a really busy commuter train. Sometimes there's nowhere to sit down and you have to stand up all the way. I find it really stressful. There are mobile phones ringing all the time, and kids listening to their portable CD players, and the sight of all those bored, grey faces is really soul-destroying. After a long day at work I get home feeling totally drained and it often gives me a headache. I usually run a hot bath, play some soft music and curl up with a good book for an hour or so, and that really helps. That and cooking – I find that all the preparation involved really helps me unwind.

Liz I've got two little boys, one's just turned two and the other's nine months old. They're lovely kids, but sometimes they just totally exhaust me! They continually want attention, whether they're hungry or tired or just bored. And I know I'm really lucky 'cos I can afford not to go to work, so I get to spend all day with them, and that a lot of mothers have to share their energy between work and being with the children, but sometimes I really miss adult company ... being around kids all day can make you feel pretty stupid ... I sometimes feel like my brain is turning to pulp. Sometimes, when I'm really tired and stressed out I just sit down and cry. When it gets that bad, I leave the kids with their grandmother and dedicate a day to my mind! Going to a film, or an art exhibition, reading the newspaper from cover to cover or maybe just meeting a friend for a long lunch and some adult conversation.

9 Law

Alistair Have you ever done any jury service?

Elena No, I haven't. Why are you asking?

Alistair Oh, nothing ... just that I've been reading this thing in the paper about how more and more people are trying to get out of it if they can.

Elena Really? I'd have thought it'd be quite interesting.

Alistair Yeah, so would I, but it seems that there's a problem about taking time off work.

Elena Yeah? What, like their bosses won't give them time off?

Alistair No, no, that's not the problem, I mean your employer has to let you off. I mean, they can't refuse to give you the time off. No, no, sometimes they might actually be really happy to let you off, you know, 'cos they don't actually have to pay your wages when you're on jury service ...

Elena Are you sure? That seems very strange ...

Alistair Well, I think it's true, that's what I've heard anyway.

Elena But if you're not being paid ... I mean that's hardly very fair, is it?

Alistair I think you get some kind of allowance ... you know, the court give you like a daily allowance whilst you're on jury service.

Elena That sounds more like it. I mean, they can't force you to do something without offering some compensation ...

Alistair Yeah ... but apparently it's not a lot ... I mean, it's much less than most people earn at work, so lots of jurors are doing everything they can to get out of doing their stint ...

Elena Mmm, yeah, I see ... I think I would too ... I mean, it sounds like a good thing to do in theory ... you know, interesting to find out exactly how the court system works and all that, but if you're going to be out of pocket ... well ...

Alistair Yeah, that seems to be what's at the root of the problem.

Elena What a shame ...

12 Words

Jeff Welcome to the second programme of Job Hunt, the series that's helping young job seekers. Last week we looked at how to write a CV. This week we'll be looking at how to write a cover letter ... and we'll be talking to Jackie Roberts ... a recruitment manager for a large human resources company based in London, who'll be telling us about how e-mail is changing the face of job applications and recruitment. So, first of all, what exactly is a cover letter? Jackie?

Jackie Well, a cover letter is a short letter of introduction written to accompany your CV. It's often the first contact you have with a potential employer and it's your first chance to make a good impression, and it can often make the difference between getting an interview or having your CV ignored.

Jeff So, what makes a good cover letter?

Jackie Well, a good cover letter is short, concise and to the point. It looks professional and well-organised. It gives you a chance to demonstrate your written communication skills. Although this may sound superficial, presentation and layout are really important and not to be underestimated. Just as you would make an effort to look smart and professional for a job interview, so you should do your best to make as good a first visual impression as possible with your cover letter. It really is important to take your time over it, don't rush it, and make sure to double check it for spelling mistakes – and always ask someone to do you the favour of reading over it for you before you send it off. It's always easier for an objective eye to spot mistakes or discrepancies.

Jeff What information should you include, Jackie?

Jackie Well, the first thing to remember is that your cover letter should complement and not duplicate your CV. It's there to interpret the factual information included in your CV and to add a personal touch. It should refer clearly to the post you're interested in applying for and it should explain the reasons why you're interested in the post. It should highlight your most relevant skills or experiences and most importantly, it should persuade the employer that they want to interview you for the job.

Jeff Jackie, you've been working in recruitment for over 15 years. What changes have taken place during that time?

Jackie I suppose the most important change for me has been the use of e-mail and the Internet: we post a lot of job adverts on the Net these days, more than we do in the papers, and more and more applicants are applying by e-mail. More than anything else, it's helped speed up the whole process. An application can be sent, read, and an interview arranged within a couple of hours. Before we had to wait a couple of days at least.

Jeff Are there any significant differences between snail mail and e-mail applications?

Jackie Much fewer than you'd imagine – obviously there are minor differences in layout, for example, you don't need to include an address, but all other letter writing conventions should be stuck to. Opening and closing the letter formally and politely, writing in full sentences, organising your letter into clear paragraphs. Not all applicants do this and I must admit it really does annoy me when I receive a short note rather than a cover letter. Some can be short to the point of rudeness – or too informal – some people even add in emoticons – they've obviously been spending far too much time in chat rooms! I'm afraid I don't even bother accessing their attachment at that point and just consign it to the waste bin!

Jeff Thank you very much Jackie. If you want to know more about cover letters, visit our website, that's www.jobhunt.com/coverletter, that's all small case and no spaces. And now on to take a look at a couple of sample …

13 Conscience

Interviewer Today, in the studio, we're pleased to welcome Janet Whittall, our lady mayoress and local Comic Relief organiser. Hello, Janet. Thanks for being with us here today.

Jane It's a pleasure.

Interviewer So, could you tell us a little bit of the history behind Comic Relief? When did it first start up?

Jane Erm, yeah, well, it first started up quite some time ago, in 1985. At the time there was a devastating famine in Sudan and Ethiopia and the charity was actually launched from a refugee camp in Sudan on the Late, Late Breakfast Show on BBC 1, on Christmas Day, to try and raise funds to help the victims of the famine.

Interviewer So, really it was launched in response to a specific disaster …

Jane Well, yes and no. As well as doing something about that very real and direct emergency, they also wanted to look at the broader, more widespread needs of the poor in that region, and indeed of poor and disadvantaged people all over the world …

Interviewer But why Comic Relief? What's the story behind the name?

Jane Well, basically it's called Comic Relief because it was set up by comedians and because it uses comedy and laughter to get serious messages across, as well as making sure that everyone can have some fun at the same time. Charities are sometimes seen as being a little dull, a little too serious maybe … I mean, obviously the causes they're fighting for *are* very serious … but it doesn't mean that we can't fight them with a smile. And it's been immensely popular. Over the years, more than two thousand celebrities have given their time and talent to Comic Relief. You name 'em, they've helped us. From John Cleese and Jerry Springer to Johnny Depp, Robbie Williams, Whoopi Goldberg and Woody Allen.

Interviewer But it isn't only a celebrity charity, is it? It does appeal to a very wide audience …

Jane Yes, it does, a very wide audience. The appeal of doing something silly in a good cause is very powerful, and it's mainly due to this incredible response from the British public that Comic Relief has been so successful. Did you know that in 1997 more than 72% of the British population actually took an active part in the biannual Red Nose Day?

Interviewer Hah, hah. It doesn't really surprise me. But how did the idea for Red Nose Day come about?

Jane Well, basically, we were looking around for a catchy symbol, something easily identifiable, but something that would also be cheap and easy for everyone to use. The traditional red nose worn by circus clowns really seemed to fit the bill – and has become incredibly popular – on Red Nose Day you can see them everywhere, not only on people's faces. You see them stuck on the front of cars, buses and even underground trains …

Interviewer So, what kinds of things do people get up to on Red Nose Day?

Jane Well, all kinds of sponsored silliness really. Some people 'Go red', not only wearing the red nose, but dressing up in red, dying their hair bright red and painting their faces, their arms and their legs bright red … and a lot of people love the sponsored role reversal events – bosses get sponsored to be a secretary or a receptionist for the day, or pupils sponsor their teachers to wear a school uniform and join them in their classes … and then, of course, there are the huge organised events, like the Red Nose Fun Run, with thousands of runners jogging through the City of London in various silly costumes, or the Big Red Football Tours, where celebrity five-a-side football teams tour the country, drawing huge crowds and raising an enormous amount of money.

Interviewer So, what will you be doing on Red Nose Day?

Jane Well, apart from reversing roles with my eight-year-old son, he's going in to the office, I'm going to join his class at school, we're holding a huge Red Dinner Party in the centre of town. Everyone has to dress in red, bring along some red food and of course pay a generous bill which will all go to Comic Relief … what about you …?

Interviewer Ah, all of the staff here at the radio station have sponsored me to shave my head and have a red dragon painted on it …

Jane Aww, hah, hah …

Answer key

1 Identity

Quotes

a) man/woman   b) man/woman

Grammar

1 a) Marilyn Monroe was born <u>on 1st June 1926</u>.
  b) It's not known who her father was and her mother had a history of mental problems, which meant that Marilyn's childhood was <u>extremely</u> difficult.
  c) Marilyn was brought up <u>in Los Angeles</u> / <u>by several different foster families</u>.
  d) <u>Finally</u> she entered an orphanage where she lived <u>until 1937</u>.
  e) <u>After appearing in a promotional campaign for the army</u> she <u>quickly</u> became an <u>extremely</u> popular model and appeared <u>on the covers of many famous magazines</u>.
  f) <u>During her life</u> Marilyn Monroe married <u>three times</u>.
  g) She divorced <u>for the third time</u> / <u>in 1961</u>.
  h) <u>In the same year</u> she was <u>briefly</u> hospitalised <u>in a mental clinic</u>.
  i) <u>Tragically</u>, Marilyn Monroe was found dead <u>on 4th August 1962</u>.

2 a) in a period when TV was rapidly expanding
  b) incredibly
  c) by Golden Globe
  d) still
  e) automatically
  f) frequently
  g) undoubtedly
  h) at the age of 36
  i) in Westwood Memorial Park, Los Angeles

3 a) Earlier on in the day I had really wanted my boyfriend to meet my parents.
  b) She just didn't answer the question frankly.
  c) Later I really regretted having asked Jane to come to the party.
  d) Normally I'd just talk to him about it.

4 a) I just can't put up with his moods anymore.
  b) The whole situation is really getting me down.
  c) He just starts flicking through the paper.
  d) It does no good bottling things up like that. / It does no good bottling things like that up.
  e) I knew we'd come up with something.
  f) It might help to talk it through with someone.

5 1 d 2 b 3 f 4 a 5 c 6 e

Vocabulary

1 a) skill b) efficiently c) competence d) fulfil
  e) satisfying f) consideration g) achievable

2 a) considerate b) satisfactory c) fulfilling
  d) achieving e) skilled f) efficient g) competent

3 a) broken off b) put up with c) sort out
  d) look up to e) talk/through f) bottles/up
  g) getting/down h) looking into

4 f / d / j / b / h / g / a / i / c / e

5 a) drop it b) pick up c) stressed out
  d) really mad (at me) e) fancy it

Pronunciation

1 a) angry b) neutral c) angry d) neutral
  e) neutral f) angry

2 Kim: I can't <u>stand</u> it anymore! Why do you <u>always</u> have to <u>do</u> that?

  Dan: <u>Right</u>, that's <u>it</u>! I've <u>had</u> enough. I'm <u>out</u> of <u>here</u>!
  Kim: <u>Good</u> <u>riddance</u> … and <u>don't</u> <u>bother</u> coming <u>back</u>!
  Dan: Don't <u>worry</u>, I <u>won't</u>.

Reading & listening

1 1 c 2 a 3 f 4 e 5 b

2 a) took off b) pick up c) slipped into
  d) sort out e) get off f) end up g) turn up
  h) look after i) get into

3 a) 5 b) 4 c) 6 d) 2 e) 3 f) 1

4 a) in my shoes b) a real pain c) freeze to death
  d) technical know-how e) sounded a bit odd
  f) worth the effort

5 b), c), e) and i)

6 a) Because he split up with his wife and she moved to the south of England.
  b) He thinks that women fuss a lot, pay attention to detail – cleaning, cooking sewing and making the house look nice and tidy.
  c) She thought that he was irresponsible at times.
  d) They camped on the beach.
  e) He likes taking them to concerts, travelling, going to football matches and eating Indian meals.
  f) Because he didn't ask for any help.
  g) Sara's best friend's mother's sister.

Writing

1 in the introduction on the first page of his first novel
2 a, c, e, f, g, j

2 Taste

Food idioms

1 a) 10 b) 8 c) 4 d) 9 e) 7 f) 3 g) 1 h) 2 i) 6 j) 5

2 a) my bread and butter
b) full of beans
c) crying over split milk
d) the apple of (her grandmother's) eye
e) as cool as a cucumber

Grammar

1 We had <u>a great dinner</u>. <u>Lucy</u> cooked for <u>us</u>, <u>she's</u> <u>a fantastic cook</u>. <u>We</u> started with <u>these gorgeous little smoked salmon pancakes</u>. <u>They</u> were absolutely delicious! Then <u>we</u> had <u>some cold cucumber soup</u> and <u>tiny little fingers of crisp toast</u>. <u>The main course</u> was incredible, <u>you</u> really should have seen <u>it</u>. <u>She</u> brought out <u>a tray of fresh lobster</u> and served them up with <u>a very simple green salad</u>. <u>I</u> thought <u>I</u> couldn't possibly eat any more, but when <u>she</u> brought out <u>the dessert</u>, <u>a home-made chocolate mousse</u>, <u>it</u> was just too good to resist!

2 a) a delicate sweet white wine with just a hint of vanilla
b) a cup of lovely piping hot tea straight from the pot
c) a mixture of tangy citric juices with just a touch of champagne
d) a glass of ice cold water with a couple of fresh mint leaves and a slice of lemon
e) a glass of fresh, full-fat milk straight from the fridge
f) a steaming cup of hot chocolate with a dollop of cream on top

3 a) Long gone are the days when the baker would deliver fresh bread to your home.
b) Up jumped the cat.
c) Andalucian gastronomy is his speciality.
d) Out of the house he flew.
e) Banking is his business.

4 a) 1 ... down went Chelsea's star player Luca Romano / ... Chelsea's star player Luca Romano went down
2 In went the ball ... / The ball went in ...
b) 1 Gone are the days when the boss played God over an office of cowering underlings / The days when the boss played God over an office of cowering underlings are gone.
2 Equality is the name of the game ... / The name of the game is equality ...

Pronunciation

1 1 A: So, what do you <u>think</u> of the <u>pink</u> <u>jack</u>et?
B: <u>Well</u>, it's <u>very</u> un<u>usual</u>.

2 A: <u>What</u> about the Versace <u>trousers</u>?
B: Um, <u>they</u>'re not <u>really</u> what I ex<u>pected</u>.

3 A: <u>What</u> do you <u>think</u> of the <u>grey</u> <u>suit</u>?
B: Oh, well, <u>typically</u> Ar<u>mani</u>.

4 A: And <u>what</u> about that <u>Dolce</u> and Gabbana swim<u>suit</u>?
B: The <u>thing</u> that par<u>ticularly</u> <u>strikes</u> me is the <u>colour</u>.

5 A: Do you <u>like</u> the <u>winter</u> <u>coats</u>?
B: <u>Well</u>, they look <u>nice</u> and <u>warm</u>.

6 A: <u>And</u> the <u>evening</u> <u>dress</u> with the <u>sequins</u>?
B: Er, my <u>grand</u>mother used to <u>wear</u> one <u>just</u> like <u>that</u>.

2 a) yes b) no c) yes d) no e) yes

3 a) certain b) certain c) uncertain d) uncertain
e) certain

Vocabulary

1 a) 7 b) 6 c) 1 d) 10 e) 3 f) 5 g) 8 h) 9
i) 4 j) 2

2 a) raw b) elaborate c) dishes d) taste e) aromas
f) appetite g) spicy h) flavours i) taste

3 a) simple, comfortable and informal / homely
b) fantastic / exquisite c) played loudly / blared out d) expensive / pricey
e) violently pushed / thrust f) successful / thriving
g) flour, milk and egg whites / batter
h) businessman with plenty of money and new ideas / entrepreneur i) customers / clientele
j) drove away quickly / sped off

4 a) 4 b) 2 c) 7 d) 5 e) 1 f) 6 g) 3

5 a) tasteful b) taster c) tasted d) tasting
e) tasteless f) tasty g) tastefully

Listening & reading

1 a) story 4 b) story 2 c) story 1 d) story 3

2 a) story 3 b) story 1 c) story 3, 4 d) story 2

3 a) story 3 b) story 1 c) story 2 d) story 4

4 a) shellfish b) being allergic to shellfish
c) the waiter d) the other two guys on the next table
e) the man from the other table f) the bill
g) the restaurant owner h) the restaurant

5
pay:	the bill, the waiter
query:	the bill
offer:	a discount
order from:	the waiter, the menu
look at:	the bill, the waiter, the menu
call:	the waiter
tip:	the waiter
book:	a table for four

6 a) booked a table for four b) order from the
menu c) call the waiter d) paying the bill
e) queried the bill f) asked for a discount
g) tip the waiter

Writing

1 a) a wide range of Spanish tapas
b) laid-back and friendly
c) no – the price of an average pizza

3 a) the latest John Howard film
b) the review was misleading. It described the
film as being light-hearted, when in fact it was
quite depressing.

3 City

Anagrams

a) Barcelona b) Mexico City c) Edinburgh
d) Dublin e) Prague f) Tokyo g) Chicago
h) Cairo

Clues: 1 h 2 f 3 e 4 c 5 b 6 g 7 d 8 a

Grammar

1 It <u>has been suggested</u> that cellular phones will be
the tobacco of the 21st century. It <u>appears that</u>
their use is almost as addictive as cigarettes, with
psychologists' reports claiming that <u>there is
evidence that</u> users display withdrawal
symptoms if deprived of their mobiles for more
than 24 hours. <u>There is certainly no doubt</u> that
mobile phone use in public is just as annoying as
smoking. Mobile-free zones are already being set
up in cinemas and restaurants and it <u>would seem
that</u> trains will soon be following suit with
'mobile' and 'non-mobile' carriages available on
all the commuter services to London. On a more
serious note, it <u>is now widely believed that</u>
excessive mobile phone use may cause cancer,
and it has been proposed that all mobile phones
should carry a government health warning
similar to the one displayed on cigarette packets.

2 b) little/hardly any c) believed/recognised
d) evidence/proof e) appear/seem
f) shown/proved

3 a) There is no doubt that smoking can lead to
cancer.
b) It is widely believed that increases in carbon
dioxide are leading to changes in the world's
climate
c) It appears that the rate of population growth
in China is beginning to decrease
d) It would seem that people believe governments
are not doing enough about global warming.
e) There is little evidence as yet that there is life
on Mars.

4 a) on b) after c) under d) in/during e) until
f) in g) during/in h) by/after

5 a) after b) sooner c) only d) never e) only
f) rarely/seldom g) rarely/seldom/never
h) barely

6 a) Only after I had left it did I realise how
much I loved the city.
b) No sooner had we moved into our new
cottage than our troubles began.
c) Not only were the local people rude to us, but
they even ignored the children.
d) Never had we imagined that people could be
so hostile.
e) Only after two months did we make our first
friend.
f) Rarely/Seldom did we see him, however, and
life was still lonely.
g) Rarely/ Seldom/Never had the children been
so quiet before.
h) We decided to go back to the city. Barely had
we put up a 'For Sale' sign when the people
began to be friendly towards us!

Vocabulary

1 a) 3 b) 5 c) 4 d) 6 e) 1 f) 2

a) tacky b) in-your-face c) soaring d) clogged
e) awe-inspiring f) haphazard

2 a) stylish b) derelict c) tacky d) dusty
e) polluted

3 a) overwhelming b) bustling c) lively
d) polluted e) stunning f) neglected g) derelict
h) stylish

4 a) 6 – handily b) 7 – eateries c) 1 – buskers
d) 2 – check out e) 5 – gawp at f) 3 – gorge
g) 4 – rant

5 a) eateries b) gorge c) gawp at
d) ranting e) check out f) buskers

6 a) mate b) joy-riding c) nicking d) flogged
e) daft f) booted

Reading

1 a) T b) F c) T d) T e) F f) F

3

Date	City	Its story
1896	Athens	The first modern Olympic Games took place
1912	Stockholm	Women officially admitted
1913	Don't know	First Olympic emblem designed
1920	Antwerp	Five rings were added to the Olympic flag
1936	Berlin	Torch relay introduced. First live TV transmission of the games.

1992	Barcelona	The first Olympic anthem to top the charts
1996	Atlanta	Approximately 2.3 billion people watched the games on TV daily.
2000	Sydney	The most successful Olympic games ever?

4 a) fierce b) prestige c) emblem d) reinstated
e) claim f) exceeding g) staging h) lucrative

Pronunciation

1 a) really b) actually c) really d) just e) really
f) actually g) Just h) really

2 A: No, I <u>totally</u> agree. It's <u>too</u> much. How could
they <u>possibly</u> expect you to put up with that!
B: I know, it's <u>truly</u> awful, isn't it? <u>Such</u> a cheek.
You'd <u>honestly</u> think I was running a hotel!
A: Well, <u>quite</u> frankly, I think you should tell
them <u>exactly</u> how you feel. That's <u>sure</u> to put
an end to it.

Writing

1 a) Furthermore b) For instance c) On the other
hand d) However, e) Nonetheless

4 a) 4 b) 1 c) 2 or 3 d) 3 or 4 e) 2 f) 3 g) 2 h) 1

---

4 Talk

Quotes

a) 4 b) 1 c) 2 d) 5 e) 6 f) 3

Expressions

1 a) 3 b) 6 c) 4 d) 5 e) 1 f) 2

2 b) talking over c) talk back d) talk shop
e) talked you out of f) talking down to

Grammar

1 a) … Yesterday <u>I went</u> b) correct
c) He'<u>d</u> be angry for a while, then he'<u>d</u> forget all
about it.
d) When he was younger he <u>broke</u> his leg
e) He'<u>ll</u> come in / he <u>won't</u> even bother …
f) correct g) I'<u>ll</u> put something down …

2 e) won't patronise f) will listen g) will answer
h) will take

3 b) used to / would play
d) never used to be picked / would never be picked
e) used to / would have to
g) used to / would run back and shout
h) would move
i) would go
j) would forget

4 a) was / used to be b) would chase c) found
d) tried e) would always get f) would smoke
g) would always get caught h) would be
i) made j) bumped k) had l) caught up
m) hasn't changed n) will still talk
o) will still tell p) will always insist
q) will usually go r) will have s) is joining

Vocabulary

1 a) conversation b) Conversationally
c) conversational d) conversationalist

2 a) very animated b) very enjoyable
c) absolutely hilarious d) absolutely fascinating
e) very memorable f) very frustrating
g) very in-depth h) absolutely pointless
i) very lengthy

3 a) mumbles b) awkward silence c) interrupt
d) aimlessly e) get a word in edgeways
f) get a conversation going g) hold up her end of
the conversation h) never has anything to say

4 a) talk of the town b) brief talk c) hilarious talk
d) riveting talk e) main talking point
f) fresh talks

5 a) fresh talks b) main talking point c) riveting
talk d) talk of the town e) brief talk
f) hilarious talk

6 a) 5 b) 4 c) 3 d) 6 e) 1 f) 2

7 a) She was in such a bad mood the other day
but now she's <u>all sweetness and light</u>
b) It's been a really hard day today. Let's <u>have a
sit down</u> for five minutes.
c) She was feeling a bit hungry so she had <u>a bite
to eat</u>.
d) All of a sudden he lost his temper and began
to <u>shout and rant</u>.
e) Did you see that gold watch in the shop
down the road. It really <u>caught my eye</u>. It's
so unusual.
f) We <u>live next door to</u> a football-mad family.

Pronunciation

Sir <u>Win</u>ston <u>Chur</u>chill was <u>known</u> as being a <u>little</u>
out<u>spo</u>ken at <u>times</u>, // and he <u>cer</u>tainly didn't suffer
fools <u>glad</u>ly. // One <u>eve</u>ning at a <u>din</u>ner party // he
had been par<u>ti</u>cularly <u>scath</u>ing about the '<u>fair</u>er <u>sex</u>'
// when <u>one</u> of the women <u>pre</u>sent de<u>ci</u>ded she could
<u>take</u> it no <u>long</u>er. // 'Sir <u>Win</u>ston,' // <u>she</u> said, //
'If <u>I</u> were your <u>wife</u>, // I'd put <u>poi</u>son in your <u>tea</u>!'. //
Without <u>stop</u>ping to take <u>breath</u>, // the <u>great</u> man
<u>turned</u> to <u>her</u> and <u>said</u>, // 'My <u>dear</u> <u>la</u>dy, // if <u>I</u> were
your <u>hus</u>band, // I'd <u>drink</u> it.'

Listening & reading

1 b) '....we can't let you in without a tie'.

2
a) He won a jeep in a competition and wanted to see how it performed in the desert.
b) Two days
c) Four times
d) Because the heat of the sun makes everything hazy and he's so exhausted he thinks he must be imagining things.
e) No.

3 a) 3 b) 5 c) 1 d) 2 e) 7 f) 6 g) 8 h) 4

4 1 g 2 a 3 d 4 e 5 f 6 b 7 c 8 h

5 a) on my last legs   b) having a whale of a time
c) put the team through its paces   d) run low
e) quench his thirst

Writing

1
a) the present simple
b) 1 paragraph 3   2 paragraph 2   3 paragraph 5
4 paragraph 4   5 paragraph 1
c) Any three of the following suggested answers:
paragraph 2 – *all day and all night, he'll die of thirst*
paragraph 4 – *as quickly as his tired legs can take him, his only thought is water, having almost given up hope*
paragraph 5 – *on his last legs, he drags himself painfully towards the main entrance, his nightmare is over, with his last ounce of strength*

2 'I've read it, I've read it'

3 b, e, d, a, c

4 *Model answer:*
There's a young librarian who's just started working in a country library. It's a quiet library and she doesn't have many customers, but she loves her job. Every morning she goes to work bright and early, sorts out the returned books, orders some new ones and generally makes sure that everything is kept neat and tidy. It isn't a very exciting job, but it makes her happy.

Then one day, as she's sorting through the returned books, a chicken walks into the library and walks right up to the counter. It stands at the counter and starts pointing at the books with its beak, saying 'buk, buk, buk, buk' as chickens are wont to do. The librarian turns round slowly to look at the chicken, not quite sure what to do, and the chicken just keeps pointing at the books, saying 'buk, buk, buk'. It occurs to the librarian that, bizarre as it may seem, the chicken is actually asking for a book. So, she offers one of the books to the bird. To her surprise, it takes it in its beak, turns around and leaves the library. The librarian really doesn't know what to think and is more than a little worried that she'll never see the book again.

The next morning, however, the chicken comes back and returns the book. The librarian is very surprised, but thanks the chicken very politely and turns back to her work. But the chicken starts pointing at another book on the counter, so the librarian gives it the book, which it takes in its beak, and waddles away with, looking very pleased with itself.

The same thing happens every morning for over a week. The chicken brings back the book it's borrowed from the day before and takes a new one. Each day the book is bigger and more difficult, but each day the chicken comes back, leaves it on the counter and asks for another. The librarian starts to get suspicious. She can't believe that the chicken is actually reading all these books. She starts testing it, giving it philosophical treaties in Latin and ancient Greek, giving it the great Russian novels in the original version, but nothing throws the chicken. Every day it comes back, returns the book and asks for another.

In the end the librarian decides to follow the chicken to see what it does with all these books. So, the next day, when the chicken has taken its book and left, the librarian puts on her coat, locks up the library and sets off to follow the chicken. She follows the chicken down the main street, dodging behind cars and into shop windows so that the chicken doesn't see her. She follows the chicken out of the village, dodging behind trees and hedges so that the chicken doesn't see her. The chicken reaches a gate, opens it and goes into a field. The librarian follows it. It crosses the field, skirts around a clump of trees and comes to a pond. The librarian hides behind a tree, feeling sure that she's close to solving the mystery. The chicken goes up to the pond and there at the edge of the pond, sitting on a log, is a frog. The chicken goes up to the frog, with the book in its beak, and drops the book at the frog's feet. The frog takes one look at it, looks up at the chicken and says ... 'Read it! Read it!'.

5 Luck

Superstitions

a) a mirror   b) a rabbit's foot   c) a ladder
d) a falling leaf   e) a black cat   f) your left hand

Grammar

1
a) The builders wouldn't have knocked down the wall if it hadn't been absolutely necessary.
b) If they hadn't knocked down the wall, they wouldn't have discovered the secret room.
c) If they hadn't discovered the secret room, the sketches would never have been found.
d) The sketches wouldn't be on display in the museum if the builders hadn't found them.

e) If it hadn't rained so heavily, they would now be living in another house.

2 a) hadn't been standing / hadn't stood
1 wouldn't have heard   2 wouldn't have hit
3 wouldn't have

  b) wasn't doing
1 would have gone   2 would be coming / would come / could come   3 would be

  c) had asked
1 would have been   2 wouldn't be   3 would be going / would have been able to go

3 a) Congratulations. I <u>wish</u> you all the happiness in the world.

  b) If only I <u>had been</u> concentrating when we did the exercise yesterday.

  c) correct

  d) If only she <u>had listened / had been listening</u> to what he said, she wouldn't be in the predicament she's in now.

  e) I wish I <u>wasn't going / weren't going</u> to New York tomorrow. I hate flying.

  f) correct

  g) I wish <u>to inform</u> you that your membership has expired.

  h) correct

4 a) I wish I had more free time.
  b) I wish I'd gone to bed earlier last night.
  c) If only I could / were able to take some time off work to go on holiday.
  d) I regret saying / having said that I'd go to the party.
  e) I wish I'd been listening to the announcements.
  f) I regret not having revised / not revising more for the exam.
  g) If only I hadn't left home so late, then I wouldn't have missed the plane.
  h) I regret to tell you that you've failed all your exams.

5 a) 'd bought b) 'd stopped c) be lying
d) drinking e) 'd told f) could have g) 'd have
h) could have i) could play j) didn't have to

Vocabulary

1 a) 2 b) 3 c) 1 d) 2 e) 3 f) 1 g) 3 h) 2

2 a) slipped off b) clenched c) flitted
  d) scrabbled about e) tailed off f) peered

3 a) make a wish b) have your wish come true
c) wishing well d) grant three wishes
e) Best wishes f) Wishing you all the best
g) wishful thinking

Listening

1 a) F b) T c) F d) T e) F

2 a) Waking Ned b) winning the lottery
c) the Republic of Ireland d) lottery scam
e) won the lottery f) track them down
g) jackpot h) dead i) winning ticket
j) the lottery all his life k) the shock
l) no relatives m) pretend to be Ned
n) lottery representative o) check the claim
p) scam

3 a) set in b) track down c) keels over
d) turns up e) dress up f) works out
g) hand over h) come up

Writing

1 a), b), d), f), h), j)

2 a) hilarious b) pace c) gifted d) sub-plots
e) subtle f) twist

3 a) paragraph 5 b) paragraph 1
c) paragraph 4 d) paragraph 2
e) paragraph 6 f) paragraph 7
g) paragraph 3

6 Mind

Mind songs

1 a) 2 b) 4 c) 3 d) 1
2 a) suspicious minds b) on my mind
  c) change your mind d) made up my mind

Grammar

1 a) I <u>feel</u> like going to the cinema
  b) correct
  c) … because she wasn't <u>listening to</u> what the teacher was saying.
  d) … he <u>heard</u> / <u>could hear</u> strange noises
  e) correct
  f) I think I <u>can smell</u> …
  g) correct
  h) This fish <u>tastes</u> funny.

2 a) can hear b) couldn't taste c) am smelling
  d) able to hear e) could smell

3 a) Having worked really hard at the meeting, we all went for a meal on the company.
  b) Not knowing the area very well, there's a danger he'll get lost.
  c) Having been cleared of theft by the courts, he immediately got his old job back.
  d) Being lost in thought, he didn't notice that his train had pulled out of his station.
  e) Not having made a very good impression at the interview, she was worried that she wouldn't get the job.
  f) Not being particularly interested in the talk, she decided not to go.

g) (Having been) delayed by the traffic on the motorway, James was extremely late.

h) (Being) intrigued by the news, he wanted to know more.

4 a) having spent b) hearing c) demanding d) having overbooked e) shouting and protesting f) Wanting g) Appeased

Vocabulary

1 a) gaze b) examine c) recognise d) dart e) perceive f) scan

2 a) admit – recognise b) understand – see c) watching – observing d) acknowledged – recognised e) remarked – observed f) meeting – seeing g) obey – observe h) knew – recognised

3 a) examined b) darting c) perceive d) recognise e) scanned f) gazed

4 a) rumour b) phobia c) nap d) docile e) addiction f) tattered

5 a) how b) come c) two d) Never e) in f) Do g) up h) Speak

6 a) make up your mind b) bear it in mind c) something will come to mind d) in two minds e) Mind how you go f) speak their minds g) Do you mind h) Never mind

Listening

1 a) Mark: his job as a doctor in an Accident and Emergency department
  Kay: her daily train journey in and out of work
  Liz: looking after her two little boys

b) Mark: he feels tense and can't unwind when he comes home
  Kay: she feels exhausted and often gets headaches
  Liz: it exhausts her, she misses adult company and sometimes it makes her cry

c) Mark: he does sport, squash in particular
  Kay: she has a hot bath, plays some soft music, reads a book and does some cooking
  Liz: she takes a day off from the kids and goes to the cinema, an art gallery or for lunch with a friend

2 a) Liz b) Mark c) Kay d) Kay e) Liz f) Mark g) Liz h) Kay

3 a) unwind b) fidgety c) get away from d) pent up e) soul-destroying f) drained g) curl up h) turning to pulp

4 a) pent up b) unwind c) fidgety d) drained e) get away from f) curl up

Writing

1 a) her final exams

b) she's got a cold, she feels very tired all the time, she can't sleep, she's eating badly, she's irritable

c) to take it easy, to go out, to unwind,

3 a) 3 b) 1 c) 3 d) 2 e) 2 f) 1 g) 3

7 Review 1

Grammar

1 a) I wish I <u>had been</u> listening when he gave out the instructions.

b) I thought the show was <u>really/absolutely</u> hilarious.

c) I regret <u>to inform</u> you that your application has been rejected

d) If I'd known that she was going to be there last night, I <u>might have gone</u> to the party.

e) Call the gas board. I <u>can smell</u> gas.

f) <u>Never have I</u> heard such a ridiculous excuse. / <u>I have never</u> heard such a ridiculous excuse.

g) Not really <u>having understood</u>, I asked her to repeat the instructions.

h) We <u>stayed</u> up all night talking things through last weekend.

i) That quaint <u>little fish</u> restaurant that your mother likes has closed down.

j) She looked <u>through the essay</u> very carefully before handing it in.

2 a) If only I'd accepted the job.

b) Having heard his side of the argument, I decided to go along with the idea.

c) She would have bought the dress if there hadn't been a small stain on the arm.

d) When we were younger, we would go camping at the weekends.

e) I wish I'd more time to spend on my studies.

f) He'll come in, sit down and won't say a word to anyone.

g) Woken by the sound, he immediately went downstairs to investigate.

h) If she hadn't drunk a strong cup of coffee before going to bed, she'd be able to sleep.

i) We wish to take this opportunity to congratulate you on your recent promotion.

j) Not once can I remember seeing him ever actually helping anyone or doing anything nice.

3 a) having hired b) reproducing c) passed through passport security d) had boarded e) not knowing f) to state g) not having stopped h) does anyone get past i) was there j) since been returned

4 a) Not only DO they expect us to work all hours during the week, now they want us to come in on Saturday mornings!

b) When we were kids, we WOULD climb into our neighbours' garden and steal apples.

c) As the problem needed an urgent solution, we spent all night looking into IT very thoroughly.

d) In the end we gave up, HAVING tried everything we possibly could to improve the situation.

e) We went to that new Mongolian restaurant THAT/WHICH opened last week.

f) I was sure I COULD smell smoke, but I really wasn't too sure where it was coming from.

g) If he HAD been paying a little more attention, he wouldn't have driven into the tree!

h) Gone are THE days when we could leave our front door unlocked without worrying about intruders.

i) It has BEEN widely recognised that stress in the workplace is increasing to dangerous levels.

j) He's a really nice guy, he WILL always have time to talk to you, no matter how busy he is.

k) I'd have said something, had I known that he'd insulted you like that!

l) We wish TO inform you that the swimming pool will be closing at 9.30 pm as of July 16th.

5 a) would always forget b) would have
c) 'll come d) 'll have prepared e) sat
f) were g) hadn't realised h) was having
i) would have happened j) hadn't talked
k) would have split l) would have done
m) had left

Vocabulary

1 a) in b) for c) In d) Under e) in f) in g) In

2 a) in two minds
b) got a word in edgeways
c) developed a taste for
d) bear in mind
e) Under no circumstances
f) deep in conversation
g) in very poor taste

3 a) I never get down to work straightaway, I always put things off and waste time.

b) Look, things can't go on like this, you're really going to have to sort it out.

c) My mum takes great pride in her garden, she spends hours looking after it and it's a joy to see.

d) I can't help Tom because he bottles things up and just won't talk about them.

e) I thought the film was great. I really identified with the main character.

f) I'm thinking of resigning. I've really had enough.

g) Listen, you're good at Maths, you tot up the bill.

h) Have you seen that new supermarket? It just seems to have sprung up overnight.

i) Your name came up in a conversation I had with your boss last night.

j) I got close to winning the lottery last week. One more correct number and I'd have hit the jackpot!

4 a) 3 b) 5 c) 1 d) 6 e) 4 f) 2

5 a) awe-inspiring b) power c) pointless
d) clench e) caramelised f) mucky

6 a) identification b) tastefully c) talkative
d) efficiency e) consideration f) boredom
g) meaningful h) unrecognisable

Pronunciation

1 1 N 2 E 3 A 4 E 5 N 6 A

2 a) A: Waiter, waiter there's a fly in my soup!
B: I'm really sorry sir, but we'll have to charge you extra for it.

b) A: Waiter, waiter there's a fly in my soup!
B: Could you just keep quiet about it sir, or everyone will want one!

c) A: Waiter, waiter there's a fly in my soup!
B: Really, what's he doing there?
A: Breastroke, I think.

8 Cyberspace

Cyber quiz

1 – a). The first binary computer was invented by Konrad Zuse, a construction engineer working for the Henschel Aircraft company in Berlin, in 1936. The first commercial computer (the Universal Automatic Computer – UNIVAC) was invented by Dr J. Prosper and John W. Mauchly in 1951. The first consumer computers were sold in kit form in 1974.

2 – a). The Industrial Business Machines company (IBM) were the first to develop personal home-use computers.

3 – c). The World Wide Web.

4 – b). New Zealand – the last two letters of the address denote the country.

5 – b)

Results:
Give yourself one point for each correct answer. Calculate your total and read the results given below.

0–2 : You are a total technophobe! Are you a time traveller from the 19th century, or have you decided that life without technology is simpler and less stressful?

3–4 : You know what's happening around you technologically speaking, but it doesn't really have you hooked, does it?

5: You are an out and out cyber buff. Watch out though, too much time spent in front of the computer screen could mean you lose the use of your legs!

Grammar

1
a) I'll <u>have finished</u> this exercise by the time the bell rings.
b) This time tomorrow I'll <u>be sitting</u> on an airplane.
c) In twenty years' time, most people will <u>be using</u> their TV as the screen for their computers.
d) By the time I finish my computer course, I'll <u>have spent</u> over 10,000 pounds on tuition fees.
e) Many scientists believe it's impossible that one day we <u>will</u> live on other planets.
f) I don't believe that computers will ever <u>be developed</u> to be more intelligent than humans.
g) Don't worry about moving to a new country, after six months you <u>will</u> have made loads of friends.
h) It's Saturday tomorrow, so I <u>probably</u> won't be ~~probably~~ going in to the office.

2
a) 'll have finished   b) 'll be   c) 'll have
d) 'll be starting   e) will be repaired / will have been repaired   f) will be working   g) 'll have sold

3
a) He won't be at home at 8.30. He'll be playing football.
b) You'll have finished the exercise by nine o'clock.
c) The good guys'll win and the bad guys'll lose.
d) He'll probably be diving right now.
e) I'll probably need an umbrella.
f) My photos will probably have been developed by now.
g) She'll be working as a doctor by the time she's thirty.

4
1   b)   after all – 3
     c)   but probably more importantly – 5
     d)   this has meant that – 6
     e)   .but now – 2
     f)   in this sense – 1

5
a) but in contrast to   b) in this sense
c) but for a calendar year   d) This means that
e) but more importantly   f) also

Vocabulary

1
a) to   b) of   c) for   d) at / of   e) against   f) for
g) of   h) by   i) of

2   1 g)   2 h)   3 a)   4 i)   5 d)   6 e)   7 c)   8 f)   9 b)

3
a) inbox   b) Graphics   c) hyperlink
d) search engine   e) log on   f) server
g) home page   h) attachment

4

```
                              ¹N
            ²O  N  L  I  N  E
                              T
                              W
 ³S  O  F  T  ⁴W  A  R  E   ⁵C  O
 U           E             H  R
 R           ⁶B  O  O  K  M  A  R  K
 F           S             T
 I           I             R
 N           T             O
 G           ⁷N  E  W  S  G  R  O  U  P
                              M
```

Listening & reading

1   Internet, television

3   a) MA   b) MD   c) RH   d) PP   e) MD   f) RH   g) MA

4   a) on   b) at   c) on   d) about   e) of

5   a) At the touch of a button
b) What is remarkable about
c) had a massive effect on
d) a major source of
e) impact on

Writing

2   a), b), d), h)

3   a

5   a) Not only   b) it also meant that   c) Prior to
d) But with   e) For the first time

---

9 Law

Laws worldwide

a) illegal   b) legal   c) required   d) prohibited
e) allowed

Grammar

1
a) He explained that he really couldn't afford to buy a new car as it was too expensive.
b) … she believes it might have been intentional.
c) You should have got the boiler checked. Now …
d) Cathy promised she would make sure all the doors were locked and all the lights switched off.
e) They couldn't have stolen the money. They didn't have enough time.
f) He can't have known about your news or he'd have said something.
g) You could have let us know you were coming to town last weekend.

2 a) would b) must c) should/ought to
d) would/could
e) may/might/could
f) would i) should/ought to

3 a) I'm really sorry, I CAN'T have been looking
where I was going.
b) She promised she WOULD phone if there
were any problems.
c) I know I really ought TO have phoned sooner,
but I was really busy.
d) His phone was engaged, I suppose he might
have BEEN checking his e-mail.
e) I thought he'd have arrived by now, he must
HAVE got stuck in the traffic.
f) Why's the light still on? You should HAVE
been asleep by now!
g) You should have told me there was no food in
the house, I WOULD have gone to the shops.
h) I'm sorry, I really don't know where it is. I
suppose I might have left it at home.

4 a) 5 b) 4 c) 2 d) 6 e) 1 f) 3

5 a) So disappointed was he with the outcome of
the court case that he decided to give up
practising law.
b) She wasn't expecting to get the job nor was
she expecting to be offered such a generous
salary.
c) He hates the fact that he has to work on the
night shift and so does his wife, who has to
spend the evenings alone.
d) Such was the confusion over the new voting
system that many people voted for the wrong
candidate.
e) So bad is his reputation for not paying his
debts that no one will lend him any money.
f) Neither was she happy to help nor was she
willing to say why.

Vocabulary

1 a) solitary confinement
b) arson
c) graffiti
d) verdict
e) speeding
f) trespassing

2 a) unto b) down c) into d) above e) by
f) with

3 1 c 2 f 3 b 4 d 5 a 6 e

4 a) 4 b) 5 c) 7 d) 2 e) 3 f) 8 g) 1 h) 6

5 1 Severe 2 Prominent 3 depict 4 seeking
5 prior to

Pronunciation

The consonants that are pronounced are in capitals.

1 a) What di<u>d</u> Tom say?
b) I<u>T</u> is the firs<u>t</u> turning on the righ<u>t</u>, isn'<u>T</u> it?
c) He trippe<u>D</u> over the wire an<u>d</u> fell.
d) I shouldn'<u>T</u> have sai<u>D</u> anything.
e) They lef<u>T</u> it down a<u>t</u> the police station.
f) He didn'<u>t</u> mean to do i<u>t</u>.
g) I couldn'<u>t</u> believe tha<u>t</u> she was innocen<u>t</u>.
h) Tha<u>t</u> was the las<u>t</u> thing he sai<u>d</u> to me.
i) He turne<u>D</u> on the ligh<u>T</u> and checke<u>d</u> the time.

Listening & reading

1 a) jurors are not paid enough for doing jury duty
b) because it's mandatory

2 a) out b) off c) on d) at e) in f) out g) at

3 a) took time off work b) at the root c) in theory
d) get out of e) on jury service f) at work
g) out of pocket

4 positive

5 a) T b) F c) F d) T e) F f) T g) T h) F

6 a) peers b) poll c) dread d) energised
e) attorneys f) responded g) demeanour
h) gravity i) mock j) riveting

7 a) poll b) dreading c) energised d) peers
e) responded f) attorneys

Writing

1 a) 60% b) 52% c) burglaries d) muggings
e) job f) 40% g) employment

2 1 a) 2 b) 3 b) 4 c) 5 a) 6 c) 7 c) 8 b) 9 c)

10 *Firsts*

Famous firsts

a) Alexander Graham Bell b) Edmund Hillary and
Norgay Tenzing c) Wilbur and Orville Wright
d) Marie Curie e) Robert Edwin Peary
f) the Lumière brothers

Grammar

1 a) whereas b) but c) However d) whereas
e) However f) Whereas g) But

2 b) I've never liked taking part in competitions,
whereas my brother really thrives on them. /
Whereas I've never liked taking part in
competitions, my brother really thrives
on them.
c) Some people prefer to go swimming in the
sea, however, I prefer fresh-water swimming
in a river or a lake. / Some people prefer to
go swimming in the sea, I, however, prefer
fresh-water swimming in a river or a lake.

d) The first time I saw the film I really didn't understand anything but the second time it was much clearer.

e) When you are learning something new for the first time, it's really exhausting. However, once you've mastered it, you expend much less energy. / Once you've mastered it, however, you expend much less energy.

f) You're supposed to think that it's taking part that's important whereas, to be perfectly honest, I get much more of a buzz out of winning! / Whereas you're supposed to think it's taking part that's important, to be perfectly honest, I get much more of a buzz out of winning.

3 a) get to visit b) got him to accept
c) got the computer working d) get to be
e) get the/my car repaired f) got them dancing
g) (we) got them to reduce h) got beaten

4 a) Let's *get going*, shall we, or we'll be late.
b) Although it was bit disappointing to start with, the film *got* better as it went on.
c) Did you know that Luke's radio *got* stolen / Luke *got* his radio stolen from his car the other day?
d) I finally *got to see* Madonna in concert after queuing for tickets all night.
e) Anita *got a degree* from Cardiff University and went on to work in the civil service.
f) Barbara is very good at *getting* other people to do all her dirty work.
g) We went to see that new comedy at the Regent. It was really good, it *got us both laughing*.
h) I *got the mechanic to repair* my old car before I sold it.

5 a) She gets her clothes <u>cleaned</u> at the dry cleaners.
b) Don't you worry, it's nothing serious, just do these exercises and we'll get you <u>walking</u> again very soon.
c) She got her bag <u>stolen</u> when she was in the cinema.
d) He got <u>arrested</u> for shoplifting.
e) The group were very quiet to start with but once the discussion turned to politics we got them all <u>talking</u>.
f) I'll never forget the time I got <u>to fly</u> a plane on my own for the first time.
g) I'm sure you can get her <u>to see</u> your side of the story.
h) Right, you have an hour and a half to finish the exam, so good luck and get <u>writing</u>!

Pronunciation

1 in<u>au</u>gurate <u>cele</u>brate com<u>pete</u> con<u>test</u> in<u>vite</u>
re<u>cord</u> <u>recog</u>nise in<u>i</u>tiate

2 a) recog<u>ni</u>tion b) <u>rec</u>ords c) inaugu<u>ra</u>tion
d) compe<u>ti</u>tion e) initi<u>a</u>tion f) invi<u>ta</u>tions
g) cele<u>bra</u>tion h) <u>con</u>tests

Vocabulary

5 a) I don't know the precise details of the accident.
b) He's a very high profile government minister and is always in the news.
c) He needs to run the distance in 20 seconds. It'll be a race against the clock.
d) Henry Ford was the first man to organise the mass production of cars.
e) He will never get another chance like this one. It's a once in a lifetime opportunity.
f) He's such an ardent fan of Manchester United that he's even named his son after the goalkeeper.
g) He's been offered a multi-million pound contract that will make him the richest footballer in Europe.

2 a) first class / first rate b) first lady c) first hand
d) first language e) first aid f) first night
g) first light

3 a / g / i / d / h / c / f / b / e

4 a) run around b) pick them up c) plucked up
d) was off e) asked her out f) springs to

Reading

1 a) on water 276 mph (444 kph), on land 403 mph (648 kph) b) 1964
c) he died d) both held land- and water-speed records

2 a) false b) true c) true d) false e) false f) true

3 a) follow b) take c) pick d) play e) pay

4 do

Writing

1 a) Sir Malcolm Cambell's land-speed record – 146 mph (235 kph)
b) not yet
c) plans to return to Pendine in August for a new attempt on the 146 mph record

2 a) 3 b) 1 c) 5 d) 4 e) 2

11 Stories

A mini urban myth

d / a / f / c / h / e / g / b

Grammar

1   a) 3 b) 5 c) 4 d) 1) e) 2
    extract 1 – The Princess and the Frog
    extract 2 – Little Red Riding Hood
    extract 3 – Cinderella
    extract 4 – Sleeping Beauty
    extract 5 – Pinocchio

2   a) 3 b) 6 c) 4 d) 5 e) 2 f) 1

3   a) to meet b) to be catching c) were going to
    run d) 'd be waiting e) would be f) to leave
    g) Was he going to h) giving up

4   a) We were supposed to spend / to be spending
        five days visiting the sights, but I was too ill
        to travel.
    b) I was on the verge of winning the contract
        when suddenly the company backed out.
    c) The show was due to start on Tuesday but
        they postponed the opening night.
    d) We had imagined that it would be very
        difficult to find accommodation, but in fact, it
        was incredibly easy
    e) They were going to catch the midday ferry, but
        they got caught up in traffic and missed it.
    f) The original plan was that the Queen was to
        visit the hospital, but there was a nurses'
        strike and she had to cancel.
    g) She was supposed to be going / to go on
        holiday over Christmas, but she was too busy
        at work and had to postpone it.
    h) I was so nervous I was on the verge of calling
        the whole thing off, but in the end I plucked
        up courage and walked on to the stage.

Vocabulary

1   a) 6 b) 4 c) 1 d) 7 e) 2 f) 5 g) 8 h) 3

    a) smartly-dressed b) good-looking
    c) softly-spoken d) fair-skinned
    e) time-consuming f) slow-moving
    g) hand-painted h) record-breaking

2   a) fun-loving b) badly-behaved c) grey-haired
    d) sun-dried e) hard-working f) strange-
    sounding g) voice-operated h) Spanish-speaking

3   a) up b) off c) off d) through e) up f) on

4   a) The whole thing was a complete <u>fiasco</u>. The
        bride was late and the best man forgot the
        ring.
    b) We'll have to <u>call off</u> the meeting until the
        director returns from Hong Kong.

c) I'm sorry that the deal <u>has fallen through</u>.
    Apparently they can't agree on the price.
d) You're going to have to <u>get your act together</u>.
    If not, you may end up losing your job.
e) We were a little disappointed by the
    performance, the dancing <u>didn't really live up
    to our expectations</u>.
f) I'm afraid the new network won't be ready
    for a week. We've come across a small <u>hitch</u>
    with the design of the system.
g) He doesn't think that she will be able to <u>pull
    everything off</u>. I wish he had more faith in
    her.
h) It turned out that the eclipse was a bit of <u>no-
    show</u>, as the clouds made it practically
    impossible to see anything.
i) There's been some <u>mix up</u> with the plans.
    Ruth should be in London and Gavin should
    be visiting our client in Manchester.
j) I don't know where he is but the show must
    <u>go on</u>; the audience is waiting.

Listening & reading

1   a) Della and her husband Jim
    b) Della bought a gold chain for Jim's pocket
        watch. Jim bought Della a set of tortoiseshell
        combs.
    c) Della sold her hair to buy the chain. Jim sold
        his watch to buy the combs.

2   a) 6 b) 2 c) 5 d) 8 e) 7 f) 3 g) 1 h) 4

3   a) scrape together b) auburn c) marched
    d) dumbly e) lock f) prized g) knick-knacks
    h) a glimpse i) apprehensive j) fumbled

4   a) lock b) scraped together c) fumbling
    d) marched e) apprehensive f) dumbly

5   a) 7 b) 1 c) 2 d) 5 e) 4 f) 6 g) 3

Writing

1   Paragraph 1 – b) paragraph 2 – c) paragraph 3 – a)

2   b

3   a) but b) too c) for each other d) unfortunately
    e) both f) However g) while h) in fact

4   a) paragraph 3 b) paragraph 1   c) paragraph 1
    d) paragraph 3 e) paragraph 1 f) paragraph 2

5   a, d, f

12 Words

Word quiz

1 b) 2 c) 3 a) 4 c) 5 a)

Grammar

1 a) wherever b) Whatever c) Whenever
d) whoever e) whenever f) However
g) whatever h) whichever

2 a) Whatever you do, don't tell him about our plans for his party.
b) Wherever I go on holiday, I always get ill.
c) Whatever time it is, whenever I go into the boss's office she's always in a bad mood. / Whatever time it is, when I go into the boss's office she's always in a bad mood.
d) Whoever is the last to leave, has to check that the windows are locked.
e) Whichever road we take, we're going to be late.
f) However long it takes, I'm going to finish this report before I go to bed.

3 a) laughing b) come c) check d) complaining
e) make f) jumping

4 a) had everyone dancing b) had the neighbours knocking c) have an expert to do d) have caterers do e) have me running around

Vocabulary

a) semi-skimmed b) retail therapy c) scratch card
d) spin doctor e) quality time f) gap year

2 a) you have my word
b) words fail me
c) a man of few words
d) in a word
e) word of mouth
f) in other words
g) I'll take your word for it
h) it's difficult to put into words

3 a) word of mouth
b) in a word
c) a man of few words
d) You have my word
e) I'll take your word for it
f) Words fail me

4 a) dictates b) snail mail c) recipient
d) addressing e) signing off
f) get straight to the point

Pronunciation

1 a) He Knelt down and asked Fiona if she wouLd marry him.
b) He was living in CambriDge, studying Psychology before becoming a jouRnalist
c) There was no douBt in her mind about the importance of leaving riGHt now.
d) They bUilt a huge siGn advertising the opening of the bar.
e) She Knows when she leaves university she miGHt have quite a large deBt with the bank.
f) If he doesn't agree with the party's social policies, he really shouLD resiGn.

2 *die:*   blind high write either buy
radio: they great page eight rain
mother: trouble enough cup does blood

3 a) clerk b) machine c) one d) friend
e) because f) daughter

Listening & reading

1 a) young job seekers
b) Jackie Roberts – recruitment manager
c) writing cover letters, applying for jobs by e-mail
d) on the Job Hunt website

2 a) false b) true c) false d) false e) true f) false

3 a) add b) do c) do d) give e) make f) make
g) make h) take

4 a) make a good impression
b) make the difference c) gives you a chance
d) make an effort e) do your best
f) take your time g) do you the favour
h) add a personal touch

5 a) 2 b) 4 c) 5 d) 1 e) 3

Writing

1 a) don't b) don't c) do d) don't e) do f) do
g) don't h) do i) don't j) don't k) do l) do

2 a) freelance translator
b) b, e, g, i, j

3 a) I'm writing to apply for the post of freelance translator.
b) I'm currently looking for a more permanent position which will allow me to improve my skills and develop as a translator.
c) I think your company will benefit from my experience and my abilities.
d) I am available for interview any time next week.

4 a) subtitler
b) solid working knowledge of English, at least one year's experience of similar translation work
c) interest in film and TV, a degree in media studies or a related discipline, knowledge of one or more foreign languages apart from English.

13 Conscience

1 a) Conscience is the inner voice that warns you that someone might be looking.

b) A lot of people mistake a short memory for a clear conscience.

c) A conscience is what hurts when everything else feels good.

Grammar

1 a) 4 b) 3 c) 7 d) 5 e) 1 f) 2 g) 6

2 a) I'm getting really unfit. I think it's time I joinED a gym

b) She'd rather spenD the weekend in a quiet country village than in a busy city.

c) I wish I dIDn't have to work today. I'm feeling really tired

d) If only there WAsn't so much bureaucracy involved in charity work perhaps then the charities would be able to get things done more quickly.

e) She wishes she cOULD come with us on holiday but her work commitments are going to keep her at home.

f) I'd rather you dIDn't do that. It might be dangerous.

g) It really is high time the government DID something more concrete to help the homeless.

h) He said that he'd rather I GAVE the presentation, as I've done it before and I know what's needed.

3 a) It's high time the local authorities did something about the traffic.

b) I'd rather you didn't smoke in my car.

c) I wish I could see more of my wife, but I can't because she works at weekends.

d) I wish I'd done something to help raise money for charity when I was a student.

e) It's high time someone taught him a few manners. He's very rude.

f) It's about time he stopped wasting time and settled down to a good job.

g) I'd rather you stayed at home and looked after the children so that I can go shopping.

Vocabulary

1 a) I thought it was rather a strange idea. /I thought it was a rather strange idea.

b) I would rather you did it than me.

c) She thought that it was rather a silly thing to say.

d) She looked rather like a ghost with her face powdered white.

e) It's better to be positive rather than get depressed about it. /It's better to be positive about it rather than get depressed.

f) Do you know the school, or rather, the college where Tom studies?

g) I'd really rather not have gone to the party last night.

h) Are you really going to do a bungee jump? Rather you than me!

2 a) I'm feeling rather tired after a long day at work.

b) I think I'd rather go away for the weekend than stay at home.

c) He's just started a new job, or rather, he's been offered one.

d) Catherine looks rather like her mother when her mother was her age.

e) I'd rather not go on holiday with your parents.

3 a) collecting b) about c) raise d) sponsor
e) event f) to g) profile h) celebrities

4 a) poverty stricken b) human rights
c) campaigns d) boycotts e) issue
f) livelihood g) impact h) habitat

5 a) issue b) poverty stricken c) boycotts
d) human rights e) habitat f) campaigns/
impact g) livelihood

6 a) a clear b) on her c) in all d) ease my
e) an easy f) a guilty

Pronunciation

1 a) 1 A: Did you <u>enjoy</u> your holiday?
   B: Yes, I did. It was great.

2 A: Did <u>you</u> enjoy your holiday?
   B: Yes, but my brother hated every minute of it!

b) 1 A: Are you doing the <u>fun</u> run?
   B: No, I'm competing in the women's half marathon.

2 A: Are <u>you</u> doing the fun run?
   B: No, I hate running! But Jim's doing it if you want to sponsor him.

2 a) A: So, you went out with <u>Darren</u> last night, <u>did</u> you?
   B: <u>No</u>, I went out with <u>Keith</u>, his twin <u>brother</u>.

b) A: Did <u>you</u> enjoy the <u>show</u>? <u>Tom</u> didn't think it was <u>that</u> good.
   B: Yes, <u>I</u> did, <u>I</u> thought it was <u>great</u>, but <u>Jane</u> thought it was <u>really</u> awful.

c) A: <u>Tim</u> told me you were <u>thinking</u> of going to the beach <u>this</u> weekend.
   B: No, <u>nothing</u>'s changed, we're <u>still</u> going the weekend <u>after</u> next.

d) A: <u>So</u>, how much <u>money</u> did you make?
   B: About five hundred <u>pounds</u>, I <u>think</u>. <u>I</u> raised about <u>twenty</u> five.

Reading & listening

1 a) to fight poverty and social injustice in the UK and the poorest countries in the world

b) by raising money from the general public by actively involving them in events and projects that are innovative and fun.

c) to a wide range of carefully selected charities

d) every penny (all of it)

2 a) Christmas 1985

b) to raise money at the time of the famine in Sudan and Ethiopia and to cater for the needs of poor people everywhere

c) because it was founded by comedians and uses comedy to put across serious messages

d) Red Nose Day

e) all sorts of sponsored silliness; wearing red noses, dressing up in red clothes, reversing roles, sponsored runs, celebrity five-a-side football

f) ordinary people and celebrities

3 c) and d)

4 a) 7 b) 3 c) 6 d) 5 e) 4 f) 2 g) 8 h) 1

5 a) devastating famine b) refugee camp
c) wide audience d) good cause e) active part
f) role reversal g) organised events
h) silly costumes

Writing

1 1 What is it? – c) 2 How did it start? – d)
3 Interested? – a) 4 Still interested? – b)

2 1 d), 2 a), 3 b), 4 c)

3 b

---

14 Review 2

Grammar

1 a) I hope I can get my brother to <u>help</u> me move house this weekend.

b) I'll have <u>finished</u> the painting by the time you come over to see us.

c) This time tomorrow <u>I'll be</u> sitting by the pool, relaxing with a drink in my hand.

d) <u>Whenever</u> you call me, I'll come and pick you up.

e) It really was frightening. The scene where the boy suddenly leaps out of the coffin had me <u>jumping</u> out of my seat.

f) <u>So</u> disappointed was he with his team's performance that he never renewed his season ticket.

g) They said they'<u>d</u> check all the details before handing in the report.

h) By the end of the night the group really got going and had everybody <u>dancing</u>.

i) He can't <u>have</u> missed the train. Jean said she took him to the station and saw him get on it, so there must be some other explanation.

j) He neither enjoyed the holiday, nor <u>did he</u> try to hide it.

2 a) The law in England recognises different types of murder. However, US law only recognises one. / The law in England recognises different types of murder. US law, however, only recognises one.

b) It's time we got going, or we'll hit the rush hour.

c) He's so softly-spoken I can hardly hear what he's saying.

d) I got John to come over to do the painting.

e) The problem with doing the decorating yourself is that it can be very time-consuming.

f) Whatever you have to do, just make sure you get it done before she gets home.

g) He doesn't really get on with the neighbours and neither does his wife.

h) He must have taken the money. He was the only person in the room all evening.

i) The government hasn't attempted to resolve the issue with the dock workers, nor has it made any plans for the imminent strike action.

j) Such was his determination to succeed that he paid little attention to those around him.

3 a) However b) but c) more importantly
d) also e) but by then

4 a) finished b) should c) could d) can't
e) would f) would g) done h) going to
i) 'll j) stood k) could

5 a) By the time we get home we'll have ~~been~~ seen most of the tourist spots in London.

b) Is that Debra's umbrella? She must ~~not~~ have forgotten it.

c) It's high time he ~~did~~ tried for a promotion; he's been with the company for at least five years.

d) I know I really should ~~to~~ have phoned you earlier, I hope I'm not disturbing you.

e) I was on the verge of ~~to~~ leaving the house when the phone rang.

f) They were supposed to ~~have~~ arrive at 10.30, I think.

g) Whichever ~~that~~ you choose, I hope you'll be very happy.

h) I'd rather not ~~to~~ have gone to the party, but I felt I had to.

Vocabulary

1 a) 3 b) 5 c) 8 d) 7 e) 6 f) 2 g) 1 h) 4

a) search engine b) first aid c) quality time
d) road rage e) suspended sentence f) spin doctor g) homepage h) urban myth

2 a) sue – not a crime / offence
b) trick – all the other words are formal
c) pot-holing – not associated with mountaineering
d) inbox – associated with e-mail rather than the Internet
e) time-consuming – can't be used to describe a person

3 a) well-informed   b) arson   c) chat room
   d) sue   e) summit   f) graffiti   g) trick
   h) time-consuming

4 a) attachments   b) confinement   c) production
   d) accused   e) co-ordinated   f) initiator
   g) expectations   h) recipient   i) sponsorship
   j) livelihood

5 a) in b) down   c) against   d) up   e) to   f) on
   g) to   h) in

6 a) was in trouble with the law
   b) live up to my expectations
   c) sprung to mind
   d) to lay down the law
   e) have it on my conscience
   f) plucked up the courage
   g) putting their lives in danger
   h) came up against a problem

Pronunciation

1 The silent _t_s and _d_s are in capitals.

   Jeff: So, how di_d_ your interview go?
   Rob: No_T_ too ba_d_, actually. They aske_D_ quite a
         few really difficul_T_ questions, bu_T_ luckily
         I'_D_ been studying har_D_ the nigh_T_ before
         and I coul_d_ answer all of them.
   Jeff: So, when will they le_t_ you know abou_T_ the
         job?
   Rob: They sai_D_ they woul_D_ be in touch
         sometime nex_T_ week.
   Jeff: Well, I really hope i_T_ goes well for you. You
         deserve i_t_.

3 ad<u>ven</u>ture te<u>le</u>pathy <u>ther</u>apy pro<u>duc</u>tion
   <u>qual</u>ity re<u>ci</u>pient pio<u>neer</u> pho<u>tog</u>rapher
   trans<u>par</u>ent sus<u>pen</u>ded

5 ad<u>ven</u>turous – _no_
   tele<u>pa</u>thic – yes
   thera<u>peu</u>tic – yes
   pro<u>duc</u>tivity – yes
   <u>qual</u>itative – no
   re<u>ceipt</u> – no
   pio<u>neer</u>ing – no
   photo<u>gra</u>hic – yes
   trans<u>par</u>ency – no
   sus<u>pen</u>sion – no